PRAISE FOR

LITTLE BOY,
I KNOW YOUR NAME

"As one of many survivors who have struggled to cope with inherited trauma, Mitchell Raff's story is both human and relatable. It pushes you to look deep into your own story, to trace the patterns of brokenness and blessings. It's a must-read for all those looking for a way forward to a fuller and more beautiful life."

—**Joey Ross**, ordained pastor and speaker

"Mitchell Raff has written a mesmerizing account of his life as the child of Holocaust survivors. His memoir eloquently testifies to the Holocaust's legacy of trauma and violence across the generations—even when memories went unspoken. Largely abandoned by his father and cruelly mistreated by his psychologically damaged mother, Mitch finds the love and stability that he so desperately seeks in his uncle Issa who with his wife Sally become his surrogate parents. But even their love proves unable to prevent Mitch from embarking on a path of self-loathing and self-destruction fueled by the abuse that warped his childhood. In this fiercely honest account, Raff shares his long struggle to break the cycle of violence, attain self-understanding, and, ultimately, even forgiveness."

—**Marilyn J. Harran, PhD,** founding director,
Rodgers Center for Holocaust Education;
professor of religious studies and history, Chapman University

"As the surviving victims of Nazi atrocities pass on, their children are left to cope. One of those children, Mitchell Raff, has written a unique and powerful memoir about being raised by an abusive mother, dysfunctional father, and kind relatives whose lives have been defined by the Holocaust. A natural storyteller, Raff uses insight and candor to draw us into a personal hell in which he repeatedly tries and fails to become the man he wants to be. At the end, he offers a ray of hope as he finally learns to deal with his personal demons and discovers love. As a first-time author, Raff writes in a fresh and compelling style, and his candid examination of his life teaches readers something about themselves. A must-read."

—**Robert Loewen**, author of *The Lioness of Leiden*

"You rarely have insight to the true story of the people you know, and you especially don't know the secrets they manage to hide successfully. Author Mitchell Raff bares his soul in this remarkable memoir of inherited Holocaust trauma. My heart ached for the losses, celebrated love's embrace, struggled with the demons, and forged forward with the journey of healing a wounded soul. In being so open, Mitch provides a type of therapy session for the reader. Hauntingly titled, *Little Boy, I Know Your Name* shows us that we can find help and support in order to choose to live a healthier life."

—**David B. Moore**, assistant vice president, Chapman University

MITCHELL RAFF

LITTLE BOY,
I Know Your Name

A SECOND-GENERATION MEMOIR
FROM INHERITED HOLOCAUST TRAUMA

RIVER GROVE
BOOKS

Published by River Grove Books
Austin, TX
www.rivergrovebooks.com

Distributed by River Grove Books

Design and composition by Greenleaf Book Group and Brian Phillips
Cover design by Greenleaf Book Group and Brian Phillips
Cover imagery ©iStockphoto.com/AJ_Watt, TCassidy, SerrNovik, Andrii Zorii, & PamWalker68, 2023. © Adobe Stock - nikolay100, 2023.

Publisher's Cataloging-in-Publication data is available.

Print ISBN: 978-1-63299-763-0

eBook ISBN: 978-1-63299-764-7

First Edition

In loving memory of Sally and Issa, I miss you plenty.

CONTENTS

ACKNOWLEDGMENTS

DURING MY ADULT LIFE on countless occasions a friend or acquaintance or even a friendly stranger would ask about my life. When speaking of my childhood, I learned to be careful in how I answered this question knowing that often it would lead to more uncomfortable questions. Nonetheless, I would respond. Eventually and without fail, my friend or acquaintance would say, "You have a very interesting life story. You should write a book."

It was never my intention to provoke such a response or write a book. I would respond with a smile and say, "Maybe someday."

Finally, while chatting with an Israeli friend named Liora, she said, "Menachem [my name in Hebrew], you must write a book about your life."

"You have no idea how many times I have been told that. Everyone has a story; who would care about mine?" I responded.

"Yours is not an ordinary story," she replied. "It is important. If you are not interested in doing it for yourself, then do it for your son." Given my son's circumstances and state of mind, I could not say no. If not for Liora, I would never have told my story.

I would like to thank my first ghostwriter, Eddie Louise, for the countless hours of interviewing me and collecting so much material to get me started on the first phase of this project. If not for the dedication, conviction, and earnest effort of my developmental editor, James Buchanan, I would not have been able to finish and publish my story. With the utmost appreciation, I thank James for helping me make it to the finish line when I was almost ready to throw in the towel.

My initial hope—beyond publication and whatever may come with that—was to help my son choose a different path for his life. After his death, I struggled with whether to continue writing or not. I decided to continue, hopefully showing others struggling with their own demons not to give up on life. Instead, if this is you, I hope you find some encouragement from my story to not only survive but find a better way in choosing to live a healthier and more productive life by learning how to deal with your demons. As a therapist of mine often said, "Whatever you may choose to do in life, ask yourself, how does it make you feel?" If the answer is not good, then why continue that path.

Prologue

LITTLE BOY, I KNOW YOUR NAME

I AM THE CONNECTIVE TISSUE between my son, Joshua, and the trauma of my parents' generation.

It is an inheritance catalyzed first by pogroms in Eastern Europe and then the cataclysm of the Holocaust.

It is a cycle of pain and psychic injury that in our fumbling manner we've each tried our best yet failed to break, knowing it lacerates those we choose to love.

Uncle Issa, Aunt Sally, my father, and perhaps my mother, in her own malignant way, believed that silence—suppressing the horrors visited upon them in their young lives—could cauterize their wounds. That this would insulate my sister, me, and future generations from the daily ritual of mass slaughter they had survived.

Suppression became just another way to damage themselves. The Holocaust cut their wounds far too deep.

Naively, I thought I could refuse this inheritance, but it doesn't work that way. Sometimes you can't choose what you inherit, and my birthright included those wounds.

Abuse beginning at age four led me to become a scared child encased in the body of an adult man wanting nothing more than escape. I became an artist of deception adept at compartmentalizing my life to hide my flaws and contradictions from the people I loved.

Perhaps no one was more deceived than me.

"You're just a well-dressed poser," my therapist Ann once told me.

Dressed in what to me was casual business attire, I sat in the vanilla armchair closest to her. Sartorially, I reflected the mien of Issa, my messiah. To Ann—a woman whose work attire rarely veered from baggy slacks and baggy blouse—I looked like a dapper man.

Most therapy appointments, I'd enter her office feeling as if I'd found Jesus (a troubling prospect for a Jew).

"I got it!" I'd exclaim.

"Explain," she'd say.

"I have the answer!" Then I'd rave about whatever piffle I believed was a miraculous insight.

When I'd finish, Ann would shake her head. "That's nonsense."

Then she'd place her open palm over her heart as a sign of sincerity. "Let me tell you, you're being selfish."

But on this day, I walked into her office feeling a storm lashing within me.

"Mitchell, how are you today?" she asked.

"Angry. Upset. Hurt."

She nodded. "You don't look angry. You look calm, cool, collected. You know what you are?"

"No. What?"

She pointed a finger at me. "You're a well-dressed poser."

"Huh?"

"You dress nicely to come across as a confident and successful man, so I'm going to call you a well-dressed poser because you live two lives. One is what people see. But in your private life, the one you don't let anyone see, you're a poser."

She paused for a moment.

"And you know what?" Ann asked. "The well-dressed poser is good at battles in the outside world, but he's not so adequate at internal conflicts. That's the person who can't cope, who chooses self-destructive ways, who creates chaos with the people he loves, who hurts them."

All true. I'd not ended the cycle, only paid it forward.

My son, Joshua, would break it on January 1, 2020.

And I can draw a direct line between that day and the day my inheritance came calling for me.

"Little boy, I know your name," she said. Her accented English was soft.

I stopped pedaling my beat-up little red tricycle.

"You're four years old, aren't you?" Her bony fingers grasped the chain-link fence that enclosed the playground of the Jewish Community Association preschool.

My eyes searched her features.

"I'm your real mother, Mitchell." Her hair was jet-black. A light summer dress hung on her angular body.

No one else seemed to notice the woman standing without a trace of timidity or unease in the alley.

She brought her mouth close to the fence to speak through one of the gaps. Her eyes brightened. A smile broke across her lips. "Would you like to come live with your sister and me?"

A sister?

"You'd be very happy."

Part One

Chapter 1
A MOTHER'S BETRAYAL

LOS ANGELES HAS PRETERNATURALLY beautiful weather that hides many of its sins.

This Saturday morning the sun shone like an early 1960s picture postcard, the sky a powder blue.

My father—Moshe—stood next to me on the stoop of a small bungalow on 12th Street. He was dressed well—slacks, button-down shirt, very much a man of 1963, before Kennedy was killed later that year. His eyes always made him look a little lost, like someone had just hurt his feelings and words failed him.

My Uncle Issa once said of him, "He's just a broken man trying to recover from the Holocaust." He said it sympathetically, but my dad never lost that expression of fear, the look that his words had failed him when he needed them most. It wasn't a lack of courage. He was just a man who could never get on top of his mountain of pain.

Aunt Sally made sure I was dressed nicely that day. In Yiddish she would be described as something of a *balabusta*. Literally translated, it's a term of endearment that means she was a good homemaker, but it also means that she was in charge of the home. She wore the pants, so to speak. And though Issa was something of a dapper dresser, the truth was that Sally made sure that neither he nor I left the house looking less than what she thought was best. To Issa's credit, he was color blind—he also had no sense of smell—so Sally was his sartorial guide.

That Sally was the boss in the house never seemed to upset Issa. He was possessed of a great equanimity that presented itself in his gentle, soft-spoken—almost aloof—demeanor. Only on rare occasions did I see Issa do more than lift his eyebrows at something that bothered him. Once I referred to a man who walked into one of the liquor stores that Issa owned as *dude*. His head turned sharply toward me. "No! Don't ever talk like that again." Loud noises could also rile his anger. If the car radio came on too loud, he'd yell, "Turn that down!" Then he'd return to the placid version of Issa. It was like sloth to roadrunner back to sloth.

The funny thing about the radio is that for fifty years he slept next to a clock radio turned to the news. This started during the 1967 Six-Day Arab-Israeli War, when the very existence of Israel was threatened. Issa and Sally listened intently to WKNX news for any updates, with Issa going so far as to place his clock radio on his pillow like a teddy bear with the volume on low. He did this for the rest of his life.

◆ ◆ ◆

It was a Saturday the day Dad picked me up. I wore a nice pair of clean and ironed shorts, button-down short-sleeved shirt, scuffed leather shoes, and my hair—a bit longer than the early '60s crewcut stereotype—was combed to one side. In one hand I held a little suitcase filled with my clothes and a keepsake or two that Aunt Sally had packed. In my other hand was a paper sack of candies my father gave me when he picked me up from Issa and Sally's house to take me to live with Mother.

I have no memory of my life before this, of how exactly I came to live with Sally and Issa. But by age four, I was living with them instead of my parents. Like Issa said, my father was just a man trying to recover from the Holocaust, and that was about as much as he could manage in any one moment. Even when my mother abandoned me at an orphanage and the mercies of the Southern California foster care system, my father let this ride. They were divorced, and his thinking was, *What could I do?*

My mother, on the other hand, was a prizefighter when it came to manipulation, quarreling, and hitting. Dad was the thing a prizefighter beats on for practice.

Issa and Sally had come to visit me in the orphanage after Dad told them where I was. I don't remember this either, but Sally—Dad's sister—told me about their visit. She said they sat with me and watched me play. Though she said it was a pitiful display of three-year-old playfulness, or lack thereof.

Like Dad, they thought, *What could we do?*

But as they left, Sally turned for one last look. She saw me sitting in a tiny child's chair, my spine bowed, and my eyes broken by loneliness and fear.

"Issa," she said, "we *have* to do something. Look at him. He's so sad."

Issa is and always will be my messiah. Sally—an emotionally hard, well-dressed, plumpish woman—will always be the person who saved me. Without her broken heart, I'd not know love; I'd not know my humanity.

Issa agreed. They became my second set of parents, and their home—barren of children—became my home.

Standing on the stoop that Saturday, Dad bent down, fixed the collar of my shirt, then stood back up.

"Give me the candy," he said, his voice blunt, stressed. It hurt that he'd speak to me like that. I handed him the candy.

This day, this sunny Saturday in Los Angeles, was just three months after I first saw my mother standing in an alley on the other side of a chain-link fence enclosing the playground of the Jewish Community Association preschool.

She'd said, "Little boy, I know your name." She did. But through her entire life, she never managed to learn who I am.

Dad looked at me, the bag of candy in his hand.

I smiled at him, nervous about what today meant.

He knocked on the door. I looked through a row of glass panes that ran vertically along the side of the doorway for any movement of their interior curtain.

"Will you give it back?" I asked.

"Give what back?" The unease was a little brighter than usual in Dad's eyes.

"My candy."

He looked at the bag, then at me. "Yes." He dipped one shoulder down to grasp my hand with his. I felt the weight of my child's suitcase in my other hand.

Dad knocked again, but it was a soft, tepid knock with the candy in his free hand.

The curtain behind the windowpanes rustled, and then the door jerked open.

Dad's eyes widened. "Giza—"

She reached out, grabbed my hand from Dad's, yanked me inside as if pulling me from a fire, then slammed the door in Dad's face.

"Giza!" Dad pleaded. "Open the door so I can give the boy his candy!"

"Get the hell away from here!"

"Giza? Please?"

I'd left one world and entered another that I could never hope to explain or run away from fast enough. My escape would take years and an Israeli court to accomplish.

◆ ◆ ◆

I've found there are two types of Holocaust survivors. Those willing to share their experience with anyone, often unprompted. And those who mention it rarely and only in brief, cryptic utterances.

My family was made up of the latter.

In the same way they never, or rarely, talked about their experiences during the war and Holocaust, they never discussed the reasons they suppressed these stories. I'm sure that speaking of the memories retraumatized them. I'm also sure they rationalized their silence with the belief they were protecting others, primarily me, from harm.

I'm sure, too, some of it had to do with how Israel shamed survivors in the decade following the war. They were often derisively referred to as *zeyf* (soap) because of stories that the Nazis used the fat from Jews they'd murdered to make soap. The implication was that Europe's Jews allowed themselves to be rounded up and killed like lambs to the slaughter. This attitude changed primarily as a result of the Eichmann trial in Israel during which more than one hundred survivors testified as witnesses on live TV, day after day. In the United States, recordings of each day's testimony were broadcast with a similar effect on public awareness, opinion, and empathy for survivors.

That such so much good could come from speaking up rather than suppressing these memories was lost on my family.

This is why I have only the vaguest outline of their experiences.

Uncle Issa was twenty-two when he ran from the encroaching Nazis in his hometown of Bedzin, Poland, only to be captured by the Russians and placed in a gulag. He spent the war logging in Finland until the Soviets transferred him to Siberia and then to a shoe factory before letting him go in 1943. He worked at a bakery in Solikamsk, Russia, until the end of the war, then fled to the West.

After the war, Issa and Sally entered into an arranged marriage.

Sally said even less. Most of what I know came from Issa.

He said she was a lively young lady of twenty-nine when the Nazis took her to the camps. I have no idea why or when she was separated from her family—six of them in all—or in which camp she was held. Nor do I know her journey after the war. All Issa said was that the Nazis used her as slave labor in whichever camp she was held, and somehow, she managed to survive.

The most Sally ever said about her experience was that it was Hitler's fault that she and Issa could not have children.

Sally did, however, once say, "Your dad would never have been capable of caring for you. He was never the same after the war."

She never told me what he was like before Dachau. I just know something within him perished in that camp.

Like his sister, Dad was a young man when the Nazis invaded Poland. He fled from them by hopping freight trains, but after about two weeks he was captured. The Nazis sent him to Dachau. And like every prisoner there, he endured brutal treatment that included starvation, standing cells, floggings, beatings, pole hangings—hands handcuffed behind his back then hung for hours from a hook on a pole so that his arms twisted back—and inhumane, forced labor. Extermination seemed like the only foreseeable end to his misery.

He once told me, "They forced us to take dead bodies and line them up five in a row on the ground. Then we would place wooden planks on top of the bodies and place another row of bodies on top of the wood. We would do this over and over. Once all the wood and bodies were stacked in place, they would set fire to them."

Hence his perpetually pained eyes and the failure of words.

After liberation, Dad came to America, ending up in Los Angeles in the early 1950s near Sally and Issa. In 1958, he ventured to Israel in search of a wife. Dad's other sister, Ruska, and her husband, Yosef—they would become my third set of parents—hosted him in their home in Haifa as he interviewed potential brides.

My mother, Giza, was the fourth young woman to present herself as a candidate. Dad looked no further, and the two were married on April 20, 1958. Mother became pregnant with me almost immediately, but due to visa paperwork delays, she spent most of her pregnancy with her in-laws, Ruska and Yosef. A few weeks before my birth, the visa came through. I was born in Los Angeles in January 1959.

Mother's story is as opaque as Sally's. What I know of it, Sally told me. She wanted me to know at least something of what Mother could never talk about. Perhaps, too, she hoped if I knew more of Mother's trauma that I'd find it in me to forgive my mother. Ruska hoped I could forgive my mother, too.

I don't know if that's possible. "She wasn't even ten years old when the war came . . ." Sally began.

Mother's parents divorced in 1935, and her father fled before the war—whether it was from the Nazis or his daughter and former wife is anyone's guess. The Nazis took Poland, and with their ascension, a Christian family of farmers took Giza and her mother in and hid them in their barn. My grandmother was not a healthy woman, so life secreted in a filthy barn exacerbated whatever condition she had. As Sally told me, "Giza watched her mother die as she lay on a table in that cold barn."

Though the Christian family risked their lives to hide my mother, they also abused and tormented her, and she never knew when their fear would get the better of them and they'd turn her in to the SS for the bounty paid on Jews.

I can only imagine what other privations she suffered in that barn—certainly starvation, physical violence, relentless fear, loneliness, hours within a severely restricted space—but she survived. Like my father, she suffered the death of her soul and a loss of any security or certainty that we humans depend upon for our physical and emotional well-being. And like my father, her wounds were cut deep. Too deep to heal.

But I can say that my father never hit me, never brutalized me.

I can't say that about Giza.

So, I don't know if forgiveness is possible.

Mother never spoke a word to me about any of it. She never tried to explain herself, though sometimes, in rare moments of compassion, she'd tell me, "Mitchell, I want to be a better mother."

There were only accidental outbursts where the past exposed itself. One day, when I was eight—before she stole away with my sister and me to Israel—we were going by bus to Santa Monica beach to visit a friend of hers, but she couldn't remember the bus stop. "I don't remember where he lives," she muttered anxiously to herself as she looked out the window, so she made a best guess. We climbed down the bus steps onto the street, and the bus pulled away to reveal a church with a giant cross next to where we were standing. Without looking away from the cross—trance-like—Mother lifted my hand in hers. There was deep concern, even fear in her expression. Her eyes watered with tears.

Silence.

"Of all the stops, we had to get off in front of a church."

It took until I was an adult to see that the cross was a mnemonic scar left by wounds that words could never adequately describe.

Another of her scars was a quiet, burning anger that would flash into violence. As was deep hatred for my father, Sally, and Issa. Everyone I loved, she abhorred.

There were endless tirades against these people, but never one word, not a single rant about the Holocaust.

If I and many others like me are children of the Holocaust, the Holocaust is a weirdly absent parent. We feel its presence but never enough to truly know it.

Most recently, I commissioned Ancestry.com to conduct research on my mother to see if they could shed any additional light on her life. Beyond the previous, I learned that she was born on October 15, 1929, near Lvov, Ukraine (at the time it was Lwów, Poland), which means she was only nine years old when the war began. In about 1940 or 1941, the Gestapo captured her father—a chemical engineer before the war—and executed him soon after near Skole, which is now part of Ukraine but was Polish before the war.

Mother was about fifteen years old when the war ended. For the first two post-war years, she was held in various displaced persons camps, then sent to Canada as a ward of the Canadian Jewish Congress in February of 1948. In many of the lists accessed by Ancestry, Mother is listed as an "unaccompanied displaced child." Though she seemed content in Canada, it was her dream to emigrate to Israel, which she did in 1950 at age twenty. Then in 1955 she married her first husband—I had no idea she'd been married before—whom she divorced in April of 1958.

She married my father on April 20, 1958.

To say the least, this is all amazing to me. I don't doubt the accuracy of the Ancestry report, but there are quite a few holes that remain. There are truths of what my mother endured—what my entire family endured—that I will never learn.

◆ ◆ ◆

About a week after my first meeting with my mother in the alley, she appeared there again. And again, it felt as if I was the only person on the playground to notice the strange woman with the jet-black hair and the same summer dress. I remember less of the details from this encounter, but the theme was the same: She wanted me to come live with her and my sister.

The thoughts of a four-year-old can be complicated.

On one hand, Mother was the woman I came home to every day, and that was Sally. That I didn't live with my father wasn't a complication. The terms *aunt* and *uncle* meant something unique to me, but I knew who my father was. He came on weekends to take me out or spend time with Sally, Issa, and me. I felt secure and loved.

On the other hand, that this woman claimed to be my mother was disturbing but also exerted a pull on me. *Mother* or *mom* means something that *father* or *dad* does not to a child. That there could be a sister waiting for me as well added to that pull.

After the first visit I came home crying. "My mommy came today . . . I have a baby sister?"

Issa's eyes widened. He looked at Sally, then said something to her in Polish, the language they always used when they didn't want me to know what they were saying.

"Mitchell, everything will be all right," was all Issa said. Sally patted the back of my head as a comfort.

Issa, Sally, and my dad knew my mother was back in Los Angeles, and they knew she wanted me back. She'd spoken with them. Her two visits with me were meant to create the image of a loving mother with a little sister waiting for me, of a life richer than what I had with my three other parents. I don't believe that she thought I'd come running, that I'd fight Issa, Sally, and Dad to get to her, but I do think she wanted to create a notion of doubt, of curiosity, a bit of a wedge.

As with any four-year-old, the culture introduced to me was of Disney and storybooks, both featuring full families—mommies, daddies, sisters, and brothers—living happily together. There weren't any Disney movies or picture books of children living with a cast of characters best described as emotionally stunted from surviving a horror of death in their own young lives.

Issa was right about Dad. To other survivors—there were plenty of them around—Issa's description of the insurmountable pain was a simple truth. But it was also a truth that applied to Sally, Mother, and a little less so to Issa.

My family was a bunch of Holocaust survivors trying to navigate life—career, marriage, parenting, love. They did very well at some things—a safe and loving home for me and Issa's business success—but struggled with others.

They did fight for me in their own way, though all of it was outside of my line of sight, as if it were a painful secret to be kept from the toddler, me. Issa and Sally worked with a social worker who said if they wanted to keep me, having a house where I had my own room and a yard would help. Issa's business acumen meant the money to do that—to finally buy a home and move from their smallish apartment—was available. Sally and Issa were also simply ready to have their own home.

Issa took me for a drive one day and pulled up to a nice-looking, if modest, house on Roxbury Drive.

Issa got out of the car and walked around to my window, then pointed at the house. "See that house over there, Mitchell?"

"Yes." A little shiver of excitement made me wiggle forward in the car seat to see better.

"We're buying that house for you. You'll have your own room. How about that?" He smiled.

I looked at Sally sitting in the passenger seat, and she smiled, too.

This remains one of the seminal memories of my childhood.

Then memory does what it does best: turns life into a montage. In my mind's eye, a moment later, we are living in this house, life moving along much as it always had, my three parents and me.

But there was more than what I've described going on in the background. Mother wanted me back. Issa and Sally didn't have legal custody, nor had they been able to adopt me. Dad was lost within his pain, disoriented by his intrusive memories from the Holocaust, incapable of raising me or effectively fighting for me. And as confident, savvy, and hardened as Issa and Sally were, the world of Gentiles outside of our Jewish bubble held some fears.

They had experienced betrayal by that world firsthand in Poland and Germany. Too many in the modern day see Germany and Poland as World War II caricatures. One is defined by Nazis, hatred, and militarism. The other by shtetls and unrecognizable, bombed-out urban centers.

To Sally, Issa, Dad, and Mother, Poland was home, like any home anyone has today. It was a vibrant place filled with parents, siblings, friends, school, play, and love. It was also a place of—if not outright acceptance and integration of Jews—tolerance. Germany to their young minds was an abstraction of a modern, cosmopolitan country slowly coming undone.

In September 1939, the Nazi invasion of Poland tore their lives apart in an instant. Gentiles turned on them in ways they—and maybe even the Gentiles, too—never conceived possible before the war.

Issa often told me, "We didn't choose. We were punished for no reason other than for being Jewish." He then would give me a hard look. "You can't forget that." What he meant was that if I turned my back on my Jewish heritage, I'd be turning my back on their suffering, their emergence from it, and the meaning of their suffering and survivorship.

Implicit in this, too, was that if Gentiles did it once, they could do it again. Yes, America is a different country, one where we feel safe, but not ever free of threat. There's plenty of hateful and violent anti-Semitism here, too. If it could happen to our homes in Poland, to Germany, it could happen here.

Issa and Sally knew that their casual agreement with Dad was not legally binding. If Mother wanted me, the courts would at the very least hear her out and likely support her rights as a mother. If, as was common at this time, the court asked me what I wanted, Issa needed to be sure of what I might say.

This, perhaps, was where Issa and Sally experienced another type of betrayal, one that was unintended but that hurt, nonetheless. After my mother's second visit, I told Issa and Sally I wanted to live with my mother and my sister. The mother I conjured was not the Holocaust survivor whose wounds drove her to anger and abuse, but a fiction drawn by the mind of a child. That I had a sister as well, the pull was too much. It was more than all the love poured upon me by Issa and Sally, who showed it in their affection, their constant refrains of "You know we love you so very much," and the home they bought and created for me.

There was no consistent attempt to dissuade the four-year-old me from wanting to follow an innate curiosity for the image conjured by the word *mom*. They seemed to understand it, having lost their mothers and fathers to the Holocaust. So, with my dad resigned to his damaged self and Giza determined to take me back, they knew that if I wouldn't or couldn't say I wanted to choose them, they'd have to let me go.

The final appeal to me came the morning my father was to pick me up to take me to Mom.

I only have memories of sunny days from this time. This day was no different. Issa came to me as I played. A beam of sunlight lit the rug and toys around me in my room.

"Mitchell?"

"Yes?"

"You know Sally and I love you very, very much. We would love you to live with us. Are you sure you want to live with your mother?"

I was too young and knew too little to make this choice. "Yes. I want to be with my sister, my mommy."

He turned and walked away. It was that simple.

From the hallway I heard Issa tell Sally, "The boy has made his choice."

I remember looking out the window. The sense that a ghost had entered the room was intense enough for me to feel it to this day.

I had no way of knowing that this marked the defeat of Issa, Sally, and Dad's fight for me.

It was, of course, an imperfect end. I wish they'd fought harder. I wish they hadn't let a toddler hold so much sway in one simple conversation. I wish Issa had explained the meaning of this choice. I wish he'd never let someone so young whom he loved so much make such a choice. But as has been said, they were all just trying to navigate survivorship, which made how they viewed the world infinitely complex.

Over the next seven years, I learned how to answer that question. It was literally and figuratively beaten into me. When the Israeli judge asked, I said, "Not this time. No way. I want out."

◆ ◆ ◆

"Moshe! Get the hell away from here!" Mother's body shook with hatred.

"Giza. Please," Dad pleaded, "I have the boy's candy."

Why is she doing this to him? I wondered. I'd never seen such anger.

"Get out now!" sprayed from her mouth, which took the unique shape of rage.

Squeak squeak squeak . . .

Mother and I looked toward the little brass mail slot. It was my father keeping his promise. The paper sack of candy pushed through the mail slot lid, then dropped. When it hit the floor, the little hard candies rattled inside the sack.

The next sound was Dad's footsteps walking away. Later in my life, much later, he would tell me I was his life's only accomplishment. I would come to know that he would do anything for me, but he was a broken man.

Mom's body was tensed, reddened. Her breasts raised then lowered as her chest expanded with air to yell at Dad. "Get the hell away from here!"

How could she treat him this way? I wondered. *Issa, Sally . . . how can I tell them to get me out of here?*

Mom spun around, her eyes still wild with hatred but her voice calm. "Come meet your sister!"

I quickly came to learn that despite these fireworks, hers was a quiet temper. Not much yelling, stamping, or raging but quick to lash out with her hands—slap, punch, pinch, throw objects at me, or whip me with a belt—to translate what she felt internally into physical aggression.

Mother led me to the back of the living room. Standing in a crib with one hand on the rail helping her keep her balance was my beautiful, one-year-old sister, Regina. She chewed softly on the fingers of her other hand, a smile stretching from ear to ear.

To translate my thoughts in that moment: *I'm here. I'm scared. You're my sister. I love you. We're both fucked.*

Chapter 2

A DISTURBED, DAMAGED WOMAN

I DON'T REMEMBER HOW OR WHEN I learned that Regina was my half-sister.

It's a bit of childhood knowledge that feels to me as if I've always known it: My father was not Regina's father, and yet she was my sister. I have always loved her as a sister, and she loved me as a brother.

What did have a lifelong impact was that our mother refused to offer Regina any indication of who her father was. The few times that Regina or I asked, Mother pushed the question away as if it were an annoying little gnat not worth mentioning.

Mother's slashes cut deep, leaving lifelong scars.

I remember Regina in her late thirties walking table to table at Sally and Issa's fiftieth anniversary party. This was a big, catered affair with more than 150 people in a large reception hall. Though Regina only knew a handful of the guests, she suspected many of them knew our mother.

"Excuse me," she'd say, approaching one or two people as she made her rounds. "I'm Regina, Giza's daughter. Do you know anything about my dad? Did you know my mom? Do you know who my father is?"

This was not a drunken woman acting out. This was an emotionally injured young woman seeking any answer to a core existential question of her identity and sense of personhood. Since many of the guests were either Holocaust survivors or in some way related to Holocaust survivors meant that Regina was not the only person in that room carrying such pain.

I don't remember any time when she wasn't curious and somewhat disturbed about who her father might be. I gave her my word that I would help her find the answer to this question. All we knew was that our mother was promiscuous—during our time with her, she had numerous boyfriends—and never committed to just one man. Regina also had my father's and my last name—Raff—on her birth certificate because despite Mother's hatred for Dad, she kept her married name.

Mom's reckless behavior rarely only affected her. Everyone within her orbit was impacted, and few escaped her anger.

It wasn't long after Dad dropped me off at age four that I realized living with my mother meant each day held the potential for instability and abuse. It also meant living on the edge of poverty where the refrigerator was empty and government checks paid most bills. These checks, of course, were often late or never materialized, leading to intermittent utilities and failure to pay rent. Mother's unmoored, aggressive behavior when landlords came by further diminished their empathy and patience.

Within a six-year period, we moved five times in Los Angeles, always into small, dilapidated apartments that felt crowded with the three of us.

I count it as something of a blessing that our first move didn't come until two years after my mother took possession of me. I was six, Regina was three, and those two years were our most stable period with her in terms of our housing.

The morning of that move dawned sunny with a specific sort of disorder in the air produced by a chaotic woman uprooting her home and packing everything familiar to her young children into boxes. Unfortunately, she was incapable of such a maneuver without falling into angry outbursts over the littlest and most absurd of reasons. Adding to it, the movers arrived early, further upsetting her mood and anxiety.

I did my best to remain invisible by playing quietly in our living room.

"Mitchell, where's your sister?" Mom asked.

I looked around, then raised my shoulders in the universal kid gesture, *dunno.*

"Mitchell!"

"How do I know? You never said to keep an eye on her."

Her expression of exasperation tumbled into anger.

"I don't know," I added. "She was just here."

"Here? Where?" Her eyes scanned the room, then the kitchen and the bedroom. After that, she leaned out the door to look out onto the street where the two movers loaded their truck with our stuff. "When did you last see her?"

"I don't know."

She raced around the apartment, then outside. I heard her call out in a tense, singsong voice, "Regggiiinnnaaa?" She rushed around to the back calling for Regina, then to the side of the house until she was back around front.

She came back into the living room, her body tense. "Where is she, Mitchell? How can you not know where she is? Why haven't you been watching out for her?"

"I don't know where she is," I pleaded.

Worry for Regina and fear for myself warmed my face.

Mother rushed outside, calling for Regina once more. Failing to find Regina, she became like a dervish and whirled back inside at me, anger written in clear, block letters across her face.

When she looked once more in the bedroom, I rushed out the door onto the sidewalk, then down the street. She was close behind, her hands snapping at me. I cut across the street to avoid her grasp but tripped and fell against the gate of a white picket fence. On the other side of the fence, a large German shepherd charged at us and then smashed against the gate barking, his blood up as Mother wailed on me with an open hand, yelling, "How did you lose your sister? Tell me!" She used her other hand to hold me down so I couldn't fight my way away from her. Her blows landed on my body, face, arms, anywhere she could pound on me.

While the dog was doing its thing, Mom was doing her thing. All I could do was try my best to fold into a fetal position as a leeward shelter to wait out the storm. I felt like a clod of dirt, something for her to kick for no reason.

Before too long, the pummeling eased into a slower series of open-hand swats and slaps. Mother's breathing became raspy; sweat beaded her forehead. She was winded by the chase and the exertion of smacking my six-year-old body.

She wound up for one last hit, and it landed hard, painfully. Soon, bruises would form on my abdomen, arms, and back.

"Go find her!" she yelled.

The movers had stopped their work to watch. Eyes wide, they stared at us. It was humiliating.

Nearly breathless, Mother noticed the movers. "What are you looking at?" She started to cross the street, then turned to me. "You better find her."

As Mother walked off, the German shepherd's barking ceased. I stood, brushed myself off, and wondered how the hell I would find Regina before our mom killed me. About twenty yards down the block was a four-way intersection. At the very least, I thought, I could stand on the corner and get a view down each street.

I scanned right then down the street to my left. About a block away, I saw Regina casually strolling toward me carrying a can of soda that looked huge in her little hands. Another block or so behind her was a neighborhood liquor store—like a small package store—that also sold cigarettes, candy, and so on.

"Where did you go?" I asked. "Mother was really worried."

"I went to the store to say goodbye to the nice man." She held up the soda. "Look! He gave me this."

"Mom beat me because you went missing," I told her.

She looked at my face, my arms. Unfazed, she shrugged. Nothing new.

I thought, *Mom will either be overjoyed or beat me again.* It was fifty-fifty.

There was a third option. When we turned to walk back to the house, we saw Mother on the street arguing with the movers. They'd finished packing our belongings—not that big of a job—but wanted more money.

"Call your boss," she said. Her Polish-inflected voice was tense but controlled. "We're not going anywhere unless you honor our original contract."

Regina and I stopped on the sidewalk beside the movers' truck.

"Listen," the guy in charge said, "that's an estimate, and the estimate was low."

Mother put her hands on her hips. Body erect, eyes intense. She was just a couple of feet from him. "I. Have. A. Contract. I'm not paying more, so call your boss because this is not what I agreed upon."

"Lady," he said, his voice rising, "I'm telling you, you got an estimate; it was low; you need to pay us the difference."

"No." Mother stepped forward, closing the distance between the guy and her even more. "Honor the contract or we don't go. You can unload your little truck."

I had no idea what she was thinking. We were essentially getting evicted by the landlord and had nowhere to go. But she wouldn't back down. That wasn't her way.

The guy rubbed his forehead. The sun was getting higher and the day hotter. He looked back toward his partner, who just shook his head.

Then he looked at their truck. Inside were our few belongings that only had to go a few miles to our next crummy apartment.

He started to say something, but Mother interrupted him. "Call your boss. You ask him."

This was well before cell phones, and our phone was disconnected. The nearest pay phone was a few blocks away.

"Go ahead, call your boss," Mother said, almost mocking him.

The guy looked back toward Regina and me, then to Mother. "All right." He knew the fastest, easiest thing was to just get this woman out of his life.

Mother looked at me. "Mitchell, you ride with the movers."

I'm not sure why she did that other than maybe she thought they'd take off with our belongings but not her son.

"Regina," Mother said holding her hand out toward Regina, "let's go."

The two of them marched off to catch a bus to our new apartment, while I squeezed in between the two movers in the cab of the truck.

The head guy started the engine and said, "Your mother's a pain in the ass."

"Yeah," agreed the other man, "she's one difficult woman."

Even at age six, I thought these guys had tried to take advantage of Mother. "Yeah, well, she sure told you."

The driver put the truck in gear. "At least I wasn't the one who got his ass whooped."

◆ ◆ ◆

Beatings were a regular feature of life with Mother and were often hard to anticipate. Rarely was I hit as the consequence of misbehavior. Often the beatings came out of the blue in the form of an open hand or the heavy buckle of a belt striking me. Always, it was terrifying and reminded me how powerless I was. This was true even if she couldn't lay her hands on me.

One of my earliest memories is of Mother falling into one of her rages, over what I can't remember, but I knew it portended a beating. I took off running from the front of the small apartment house where I was playing and darted inside to find a place to hide. In the kitchen, I crawled into a lower cupboard, closed the door, and tried to calm my breathing so she wouldn't hear.

"Wait until I get my hands on you," she said as she came through the door into the kitchen. There was a threatening calm to her voice, a signal of Mother's deep anger.

She paused. "Where are you?" Her voice wasn't raised in fury. It held a coolness that my child mind knew would lead to her hurting me. I cowered in my hiding spot, praying she wouldn't find me.

Then I heard her shoes scuff out of the kitchen. "Where the hell are you?" she said as she paced through the apartment. "Wait until I get hold of you!" Her voice finally betrayed the depth of her anger. Eventually, her rage ebbed, and I could emerge from my hiding spot as if nothing had happened.

Other times, the fury rose quickly, catching me by surprise. There was the time we were walking down the street when I laughed at something a friend said to her. Mother turned and slapped me, hard.

"You think that's funny?" she asked.

I held my hand against my reddening cheek, a mix of pain and humiliation.

She also had little patience for sleepiness.

"Time to get up," she once said from the edge of my bed.

I lifted my body but not much else.

"Time to get up," she said again.

Still, I was tired and slow. In the next moment, the whip of a belt lashed against my thigh, leaving a long linear red mark.

"Now are you going to get up?"

Merely standing near her held the risk of being slapped or pinched as a way for her to let out her anger. Most of the time I never knew the cause. It could be me or an intrusive memory from the war. I had no way of knowing. It was always painful, both literally and emotionally. When it happened in front of others—as it often did—my mother's physical abuse was also humiliating.

Later, I would learn that such humiliation made up much of my family's experience during the war. It wasn't only the constant specter of death and torture that haunted them, but the sense of the inferior nature of their existence. Humiliation was an indelible stain on their psyches, of being considered unworthy and undeserving of respect, compassion, or life itself—the sense that they were inconsequential to the universe. As an adult, I came to partly understand my father's silence, Sally and Issa's careful maneuvering around their memories of those days as if trespassing in a minefield, and my mother's rage at the world.

It doesn't excuse my mother's abuse or how Sally, Issa, and my father allowed me to leave their safe, loving home for hers. But maturity and the little breadcrumb clues they left as to their collective trauma and suffering during the Holocaust make it all at least understandable.

As a child, though, I had to wonder if the abuse was my fault. Issa had given me the chance to choose him and Sally, but I said no. I needed to fill a void that only a mom can fill. That a baby sister came with it sweetened the deal. I was also a rambunctious boy with ADHD who didn't do well at school. Lacking the insight and maturity of an adult, it was too easy for me to blame myself, with the effect of lowering my already low self-esteem.

It also didn't help that I looked a lot like my father. I've wondered for a long time if this was one of the reasons why Regina so rarely found herself at the receiving end of Mother's temper. As a child, I interpreted this difference between our treatment to mean that I was a bad kid.

No matter the cause, the persistent threat of physical abuse caused me to live in a constant state of fear and hypervigilance. Around age five or six, I slipped into a survival mindset where I did all I could to anticipate the next outburst, to stay a step ahead of Mother to avoid the next punch.

It never worked. She was a disturbed and damaged woman with a lot of stress, and I never knew what would happen one moment to the next.

As my later life would show, once you get used to living in a continual state of chaos, it's hard to simply let it go.

Chapter 3

ISSA THE *TZADIK*

BY AGE NINE, MY PRESENCE frequently frustrated and tired Mother, until one night she snapped in a way she'd not done before.

Life with her held few highlights. Ed Sullivan was one. The Beatles were to perform on this particular evening, which meant that watching was an imperative for anyone younger than about eighteen. So, when Mother told me to turn off the TV, take a shower, then get to bed just as Sullivan walked onto the stage, I wasn't having it.

"Mitchell!"

"Mom!"

That was all it took. She grabbed me by the scruff and tried to drag me. I fought back, broke free, but couldn't move fast enough to get away. She smacked me with the open palm of her hand, then twisted her fingers into my hair. With her free hand, she grabbed hold of a belt loop and hoisted me to my feet. I tried to twist and wiggle out of her grasp, but I wasn't yet strong enough to outfight her.

Like a bouncer running a drunk out of a bar, she bum-rushed me outside on the front steps, then slammed the door shut and locked it. Our fifth—and what would be our final—Los Angeles apartment was on the first floor of a small fourplex on Chariton Street, a small dogleg of a street not far from the Santa Monica freeway.

"Don't, Mom! Please! I'll be good! I promise!"

Nothing doing. The door remained closed and locked. For emphasis, Mom turned off the porch light. She'd thrown me out like a piece of trash and wasn't going to let me back in.

What do I do now? I thought. It was after eight at night, and the air was chilly. I walked around back of the apartment where there was a small, unlocked washroom with a water heater. Spider webs draped the ceiling and spaces around the water heater, and next to it was an old-style washing machine with a rolling pin to wring water from clothes before they were hung outside on a clothesline. There was a sour odor of dampness like in an old, wet basement. I didn't see any, but I could envision rats hiding in the shadows. I wondered what was so wrong with me that I deserved to be treated in this way. And then I felt a deep shame again and regret that I'd chosen Mother over Issa and Sally.

The next morning, I climbed back in the apartment through the back bedroom window.

A few weeks later, nearly the same thing happened. I talked back or was bouncing around the apartment with too much energy—I can't remember—when she grabbed me by my hair and shirt collar. Knowing what was coming, I fought back and pleaded, "Mom! No! Please!" but nothing I said broke through her anger. She tossed me out on the steps like a sack of potatoes.

A chilly rain was falling, so I tromped through wet grass to the washroom. I spent the night with my body leaning against the door staring at the faint light from the water heater's pilot flame. I shivered with fear and cold, thinking that the bogeyman would get me.

Telling this story now, I can't help but think of Mother as a young girl about my age forced to hide in that barn during the Holocaust. In particular, I imagine her sitting alone with the rats and farm animals the first night after watching her mother die. It must have been terrifying and lonely. What did they do with her mother's body? I can also imagine that since hiding a Jew would mean certain death for the family that during the day, they forced her to hide for prolonged periods in a small space without light, away from prying eyes. How many times was she hiding as neighbors visited or German soldiers came to steal whatever food the farm produced for the war effort? I'm sure, too, that she often wondered what kept the Christian family hiding her from turning her in for the bounty paid by the Nazis for Jews. What could Mother offer them that was more valuable than the lives of that family?

I know that survivors like my dad, Sally, and Issa wanted to shield the next generation from such horrors and promised to never let their children suffer as they had. For a survivor like my mother, she probably thought, *If I could do it for years, he can do it for a night.* Almost as if she wanted to have some morsel of the unfairness of her life during the war visited upon me, a child whom she viewed as yet another tormentor.

This then always leads me to the thought, *Why keep me? Why not just let me go home to Sally and Issa?*

I've always had more questions than answers, but after these nights alone in the washroom, I started to seek as much time away from her grasp as I could. Mostly, this took the form of wandering the relative safety of the streets—especially alleyways—near our apartment like a nine-year-old derelict. Often, I'd find hidden treasures in trash cans filled with discarded items or things lying in an alley that to my young mind held immense value and interest.

Once I found an electric train set. When Mother saw me setting it up and I told her where I'd found it, she shrugged and said, "It amazes me what people throw away. It really is a shame." Another time I brought home a discarded Christmas tree. Mother eyed it like a sociologist inspecting an artifact, then smiled. "It's pretty," she said. For a time, it brought a bit of calm into our home. Perhaps there was a pleasant memory associated with this most Christian of holidays. Or maybe it added a bit of color and light to what was a dim and impoverished life. Not long before finding the tree, we'd been walking home from an A&P grocery store one block from the apartment when Mother stopped. She held a brimming bag of groceries in her arms for which she'd paid about twenty dollars. In the A&P she'd been pissed, complaining to the check-out girl, "This is all I get for twenty dollars?" To me, it was a magnificent amount of food.

I followed Mother's eyes down the block to a utility truck parked in front of our apartment. "There's a man over there, and I owe him money," she said. "Let's stop here and wait for him to go away." Not long after, the truck pulled away—the coast was clear.

During one of my alley runs around the neighborhood, I found a dirty magazine. Nothing too salacious—like a *Playboy* without the articles—but I'd never seen such a thing. The women's bodies were beautiful and fired an insistent curiosity. Though I knew little of sex and the meaning of this magazine, I knew enough to keep its existence a secret from Mother. Hidden beneath my mattress, I visited its pages often and enjoyed the peculiar sensation the photos provoked, a sensation I'd experienced once before.

Prior to Issa buying the house where I had a room and a backyard to play in, we lived in a modest apartment in a building with a set of stairs that I liked to wander up and down. The tenants knew one another, and on hot days—this was before air conditioning became common—people left their doors open for the breeze. They became used to the four-year-old me bouncing and humming as I wandered up and down the stairs to explore the building. One neighbor in particular, a middle-aged woman who lived alone, became fond of me, and I of her. Sometimes she gave me little gifts, such as a blue tin cup and another time a shaker with a lid for mixing Ovaltine with milk. I loved both gifts, and I'm sure Sally let the woman know that she set one or the other at the breakfast table for me every morning.

One day I wandered into her apartment and found her in the kitchen.

She turned toward me with a smile. "Hello, Mitchell. I'm baking cookies. Would you like one?"

She wore only a skirt and bra, which I thought was strange. "Why are you wearing a—"

"I'm hot," she interrupted, then laughed like I'd asked a silly question.

She dotted a baking sheet with small globs of cookie dough and placed the tray in the oven. She turned to me, widened her eyes, and reached out her hand. I took it. She guided me into a room adjacent the kitchen with a small bed, then lifted me onto the bed.

"Lie back, Mitchell," she said, smiling.

She pulled my pants and underwear down and started fondling my penis.

Later in life, I told this story to my therapist Ann. One of the issues Ann and I wrestled with was my habit—perhaps a form of addiction—of visiting illicit massage parlors. When I finished describing what happened with the upstairs woman, I added, "This is not an unpleasant memory for me, and I hold no resentment toward her."

"Wait a minute. You what?" Ann asked.

"I really do not have any issues about it," I replied.

She sat forward in her chair. "You have no feelings of anger or disappointment with this woman?"

"No. None."

"How would you feel if this happened to your son?" Ann asked.

I paused for a moment. "Well, of course I'd be upset and disturbed by it. I'm not saying what she did was right or acceptable. It was totally wrong of her, but for whatever reason, it doesn't bother me. As best as I can tell, I really don't care."

The whole thing seemed so benign and pleasant. The upstairs woman chatted idly with me as she fondled my penis—about what I can't remember—and I chatted idly back. Her eyes roamed from mine to her hand, then back to mine, and her smile was comforting. After a few minutes she asked, "Is this hurting you, Mitchell?"

"No." I felt no fear or discomfort.

"Is what I'm doing bothering you? Tell me if it is."

"No, I don't mind." I didn't want to hurt her feelings or think that I didn't like her.

A few minutes later, she said, "I think this is bothering you. Maybe we should stop."

"Okay."

"Stand up, Mitchell."

I did, and she pulled my underwear and pants up.

A day or two later, I sat with Sally and Issa eating breakfast in our kitchen.

"I want to go visit the lady upstairs," I announced.

"No, Mitchell," Issa said. "You will not be visiting her anymore."

That was it. I don't remember, but I must have said something to Sally or Issa, probably Sally. There wasn't a big deal made of it, and no one ever told me that the neighbor had molested me. I just couldn't visit her ever again, which hurt because I liked her. A few weeks later we moved to the new house, and a few weeks after that, maybe six weeks to two months, Dad took me to live with Mother.

In the session with Ann when I explained how I felt about it, she'd said, "Maybe you thought her affection was unconditional, like a mother's."

This may be true. At age four, I knew that I wanted to know my mother and wanted to live with her. It was a hole in my life that was no different from Regina in her late thirties wandering through a party asking each person, "Do you know who my father is?" Not having a father disturbed her throughout her life. Not having a mother disturbed me until age four. Of course, if Regina's father was anything like Giza, she would've wanted to run far, far away, too.

Whatever the reason, the upstairs neighbor brought a sense of comfort.

◆ ◆ ◆

There was never a day that I didn't have to navigate Giza's anger and my persistent sense of hypervigilance—an unceasing loop of fight, freeze, or flight. But that didn't mean there weren't moments when Mother acted like the mom she'd promised to be when she said, "Little boy, I know your name."

The most memorable occurred a month or two after I'd found the magazine with the naked women. I'd just turned ten and was sitting on my bed struggling to put together a model car from a kit when I became disgusted with the uncooperative plastic pieces and threw it down with a loud "Damn it!"

"What are you trying to do?" Mother asked as she walked from the kitchen into the living room, drying her hands on her apron. The Chariton Street apartment was so small that my bed occupied a corner of the living room.

"I'm trying to put this stupid thing together, but I can't figure it out!"

She sat on the side of my bed. "Put it away for now and give it a rest. You'll be better at it when you come back to it." Her manner was soft and calming, a motherly side of her personality I rarely got to see.

Her tenderness so moved me that, without thinking, I said, "I have something I want to show you."

I pushed the model out of the way, stepped off the bed, lifted the mattress, and showed her the magazine. It felt so good to have the mother I needed that I wanted to reciprocate her kindness as a way to make it last.

She eyed the magazine, smiled, then gave me a look of amused endearment. "These pictures interest you?"

I nodded.

"Okay," she said. "Good for you."

Then she stood and walked back into the kitchen.

◆ ◆ ◆

After our iconic preteen moment, things went back to normal. I'm not sure if it was the next day or the day after, but she smacked me across the face in front of our apartment. For what? I didn't know then and I still don't now. It was just one more round in her endless internal war between love and resentment.

Desperate to re-conjure the good mother, I swept and mopped the floor the next day. When she got home, rather than thanking me, she beat me with the belt. "I did a good thing!" I cried. "Why are you so angry?"

She didn't have an answer. Just one last whack on my back.

As part of the agreement that sent me to live with Mother, my dad got to see me every other Saturday. Most of the time, he just wanted to hang out with me, which I didn't mind, but I much preferred it when he took me to Sally and Issa's. I loved seeing them, they loved seeing me, and there was food.

"Mitchell," Issa said, pointing to a bruise on my arm. "What's that?"

I shrugged, too embarrassed to tell him the truth. Issa nodded, then looked at Sally.

A few days later, I saw Issa parked on the side of the street in his white, four-door Buick Skylark. He stepped from the car. "Mitchell, it's wonderful to see you."

"Issa!" I said, truly happy and surprised to see him.

He nodded at the bruise on my arm. "How are things with your mother?"

I couldn't lie to him, and as I write this, I now know that he had been aware that Mother was beating me for quite a while. "Mom hit me with a belt again."

He shook his head. "How's your sister?"

"She's good."

"Okay." His gestures were gentle, his voice soft spoken. "So, your mom's hitting you."

He said this more as a statement of fact than a question. I nodded.

"I'm sorry."

"It's okay."

"No, Mitchell, it's not." He paused for a thought. "Are you hungry?"

"I am."

"Why don't you hop in, and we'll get something to eat."

Issa drove us to McDonald's, where he encouraged me to order whatever and as much as I wanted. I asked for two cheeseburgers, large fries, and a Coke.

"That's all?" he asked.

"That's all."

Issa and Sally were no longer in my life every day, but I saw them frequently enough for Issa to know how much I could put away. As with the beatings, he'd suspected—really, he knew—there wasn't enough food at Giza's. And it wasn't like he and Sally weren't doing what they could to help. He bought the mattress I slept on and had paid for me to go to sleepaway camp the previous summer. He also knew these were the few things that Giza would allow him to buy for me. She said no to Issa far more than she said yes.

"You can order something else if you want," Issa said.

"No, thank you."

"What do you eat at home?" he asked after we sat down.

I shrugged.

"Come on, Mitchell. Use your words."

I felt humiliated but wanted to honor Issa with the truth. "Regina and I ate raw bacon yesterday because we couldn't find anything else to eat."

"Bacon?" His eyes winced.

Regina and I were starving. That there was bacon in the refrigerator was something of a minor miracle. Most days all we had was some sugar to put in water.

He sensed my embarrassment, and for the rest of the meal we talked about nothing much in particular. It was just so good to be with him, to have run into him like this. I felt safe and protected.

When I finished eating, he said, "Let me take you home." We got in the car, but he knew better than to pull up to the house, so he stopped a block or two away.

"Thanks, Issa!" I said as I opened the door.

Before I could climb out of the car, he bumped my shoulder with his hand. In his palm was a small pile of coins. He looked at me and lifted his hand to indicate, *here, take a few*. I picked out a quarter and a dime. He lifted his hand again, *take more*. I picked out a few more quarters.

"Mitchell," he called out as I walked away.

I turned.

He leaned his head out the window. "You know Sally and I love you very, very much."

The next afternoon after school, I heard a car pull up, a car door open, and then a few seconds later the door slammed shut and the car pulled away. I looked out, and there on the stoop were two bags of groceries. When Mother came home, she asked where they materialized from, though she already knew. I kept my head down.

"Mitchell!"

"I don't know," I said. "I didn't see who it was."

A few days after, the white Buick Skylark pulled up next to me in front of the A&P.

"Issa!"

"Mitchell, how are you?"

Like before, he asked if I was hungry. Knowing there was a burger, fries, and a Coke in the offing, I said of course. He then told me, "Mitchell, listen, make sure you walk to and from school the same way, okay?"

"Why?"

"I keep missing you."

How dumb, I thought, *of course*. Each day I'd hoped to run into him again, but never took the same route home to or from school. *What a dummy not making it easier for him to find me!*

A few days later, more groceries landed anonymously on our stoop. Mother asked where they came from, but all I could do was shrug.

Her eyes communicated that she wasn't buying it for a second.

Mother picked up the phone, dialed. "Issa, no more groceries." Her voice was angry but controlled. "I don't care. No more."

Issa must have pleaded that we were hungry.

She put down the phone, and that ended the groceries.

But that didn't stop Issa from looking for me.

"Mitchell," he said, stepping out of the Skylark. He seemed a little agitated. "How are things with your mother?"

"They're okay."

"No, Mitchell. The truth." He let a beat pass. Worry inflected his eyes. "Don't you remember what you told me? Let me see," he said. "Lift your shirt, Mitchell. Please, let me see. It's all right."

I was unsure what to do. I remained still and silent.

"The marks on your stomach and back—how are they healing?"

"What marks?" I was truly unaware.

"You don't remember what your mother did to you?"

"No."

"What do you mean you don't remember?"

I hunched my shoulders.

He bent his body and reached a hand toward me. "Let me see. Lift your shirt, please."

He looked at my back and abdomen. His eyes winced as they usually did when he saw or heard something that caused him pain. As he examined me, he explained that a week ago, I'd told him what Mother had done to me and showed him the deep purple and black bruises.

He lowered my shirt then stood up. "It's much better now," he said, relieved. "You told me she had done it with a belt, with the buckle. I've been looking for you for the past few days to be sure you're all right."

As an adult working with Ann, I'd learn that a common response by children is to enter a state of dissociation, which can take on a few different forms. One is to block out the traumatic event. Another is to slip into a vague state of mind where everything feels as if it's a dream and one is removed from what is happening to them. In this instance, I'd blocked out the beating and entered that fluid, dreamy state with Issa. These strange states of being were common for me, and I wonder how much of my life with Mother I can't remember, or that now seems like dreams rather than memories.

I imagine, too, that the same was true for my family. Their memories of the Holocaust could have been riddled with missing spaces or ones that were so dreamlike it was hard to tell if they were real. My mother being the youngest at the time, maybe she dissociated so much that she didn't have the recall to fully prompt her empathy. I don't know.

What I do know is that in Hebrew the word *Tzadik* means "Righteous One." Tzadiks are people of exceptional heart and kindness whose lives are a blessing to those around them. I've never held any doubt that Issa in his simple, well-spoken, emotionally full way was for me a Tzadik.

"Let's go get something to eat," Issa said. He placed his hand on my shoulder to guide me to the car.

He dropped me off a block or two from Mother's apartment. "You know Sally and I love you very, very much."

"I do. I love you, too."

I decided right then that I had to find my way back to Issa and Sally.

Issa and Sally wanted me back, too. They just hadn't let me in on the plan.

Chapter 4

RUNNING

I'VE NOT TOLD MY STORY to a lot of people, but when I do, they tell me it should be a book. "No, a movie!" they add.

Okay.

When I describe running away, they ask, "What was the last straw?"—like there was some final abuse that pushed me out the door. There was no last straw, no particular beating or humiliation. It was a combination of needing love and knowing that I'd had enough.

Issa and Sally showed me that they loved me. Mother showed me that her love for me was painful and perverse. The spark was that I wanted to be loved, and when I woke up to that fact, I left my mother early one spring morning in 1969. I was ten years old.

Sally and Issa lived just five miles away, and I knew the way. I'd lived there for a few months, after all, and had been there with my dad numerous times. I also knew, or at least felt confident, that they'd open the door and embrace me. I was coming home, finally.

When Sally opened the door, her eyes widened.

"I don't want to live with Mother anymore!" I cried.

Sally, Issa, and my dad gave me the choice at age four as to whom I wanted to live with. Well, I took that choice back. A do-over.

"Mitchell?" Sally said.

"She hurts me!" What more reason could I give?

"Come in, come in . . ."

Issa was not home. He was working at his liquor store.

Sally brought me into the kitchen and offered me a sandwich, chips, and a 7UP, which I happily accepted. Then she called Issa and they spoke softly in Polish as I ate.

Food and being in Sally and Issa's home calmed me. Sally told me that she loved me but added that she wasn't sure what to do. Thinking about it now, she and Issa had already involved a social worker with child services and a lawyer, all of this happening without my knowledge. Mother knew they were working to regain custody in Dad's name, deepening her already considerable hatred and resentment of them. I knew nothing of it. I imagine, too, that my sudden and unexpected presence in their home added a complication. *Does this help our case? Hurt the case?* I'm sure they wondered as they spoke on the phone. *What should we do?* I know they wanted me to stay, to protect me from the beating I would get for running off like this.

Then the doorbell rang. Sally's brows creased with worry. This wasn't expected.

She went to answer it. There was a mumble of voices, but I clearly heard Sally say, "Yes, come in."

It was Mother with a pair of police officers.

In a panic, I ran from the kitchen into Issa and Sally's bedroom and hid in a tiny closet. A moment later, Sally opened her closet door. The two police officers stood behind her. Mother remained on the front stoop, unwilling to walk across the threshold into Sally and Issa's home.

Mother felt empowered and vindicated. The police and the law were on her side.

That was it. No discussion. No chance for me to plead my case to the cops.

As we walked out the door, Mother turned to Sally and said, "You're a witch!" It was her favorite epithet, as if the ten-year-old girl hiding from the gas chambers in a barn had never grown up.

"You belong to me, Mitchell," she said on the way home. "To me, Mitchell. No one else. Me."

I was a possession. One that I believed she didn't want and wouldn't ever let go of or stop hitting. She wasn't like any other mom I'd ever seen.

◆ ◆ ◆

If nothing else, my escape attempt prompted Issa, Sally, and Dad to move faster. They believed each day with Mother was yet another day she cut deeper wounds, that my safety and well-being were at risk. With Mother's unpredictability and volatility, no one knew what she was capable of or might do in reaction to attempts to remove me from her home.

She was a disturbed woman with no bottom and no off switch.

This was the context that child protective services ordered Mother to bring me in for an interview. This was also the first I learned of the attempt to bring me back to Sally and Issa. During one of Issa's visits with me in his Skylark, he told me that he and Sally wanted me back, that the child protective services interview was part of that effort, that he was hopeful, and that I should tell the truth during the interview.

Issa's advice was much easier to remember than the lies Mother coached me to tell while we took a series of buses to get to the downtown location of the interview.

"I know what's going on," she ranted. "Sally, that witch, and Issa want to take you away from me. There's a court case coming, and this lady today is going to ask you a bunch of questions."

Mother was in a state of mild incoherency. Part of it was due to the stress that she might lose custody of me, and another part was due to her recent hepatitis C diagnosis. For months, the hepatitis caused severe itching so that she used forks to scratch at her scalp, arms, and back. The fork's tines left bloody, red streaks on her skin that scabbed and were slow to heal and quick to become infected due to the hepatitis. The sight of Mother scratching herself with a fork was like a dog gnawing at fleas. She made me eat every meal with a spoon.

At the time, doctors could treat the symptoms (not that well), but they could not cure the disease or do more than slow its progression. It's hard for me to say when Mother began to unravel, but her slow-motion collapse was picking up pace.

We were sitting at the back of the bus, driver's side. Mother spoke directly to me, her eyes tightly on mine, body hunched over me like a hood. "You need to answer the questions correctly, in my favor, or else they'll take you away from me. I know they will. So, whatever you say has to be positive, that I'm treating you nicely, that things are good at home. Whatever you do, don't say things that make me look bad."

She then began to script my answers to specific questions.

Who is this person? I thought. *How could she not know that I want to be away from her?*

But at the same time, I had conflicting emotions. Her behavior and the tension in her voice made me afraid. *What if I tell the truth and she finds out?* Perhaps the most disorienting emotion was an odd sense of loyalty toward Mother, as if by telling the truth I'd be betraying her.

I felt like I was walking a tightrope. At the same time, I knew I'd have to be an idiot to listen to Mother and sabotage myself. I desperately wanted Issa and Sally.

I'm sure Mother didn't *know* I was meeting in secret with Issa, but I'm also sure she suspected it. She was a woman taught by the Holocaust to mistrust, and she had an innate, cagey intelligence. Soon after the summons for the interview arrived—Mother already knew a court date would be coming not long after the interview—she stopped letting me out of the house.

"You cannot leave this house."

"Mom, I want to play. Everybody's outside," I complained.

"No," she said with clear finality. She walked away mumbling, "I don't want you talking to anyone."

Issa still found me on my way to or from school. He told me about how the court case was developing and reemphasized that I should tell the truth in the interview.

"In a few weeks, we'll be in court, Mitchell," he said. "I'm hopeful."

Mother suspected this may be happening, so she stopped me from going to school, too. One day, she saw me standing in front of a window watching the other kids in the neighborhood play.

"Step away from the window, Mitchell," she said. "People will think something's wrong with you."

◆ ◆ ◆

Mother waited in a reception area outside the interviewer's office. Inside, I sat in front of a desk in a small, modest office. There were no toys or games or decorations of any kind. It was a bureaucrat's office straight out of central casting. The social services woman also looked as if she came right out of central casting: She was middle-aged, efficient, and cold.

"How often do you have clean underwear?" she asked.

"Most of the time but not always."

Her head nodded as she wrote a note.

"How many meals a day do you eat?"

"When I see my Uncle Issa, two. Most days there isn't enough food. One time, Regina—that's my sister—and I ate raw bacon because that was all we could find."

She jotted more notes. "Does your mother ever spank you?"

"No. She beats me, sometimes with her open hand and sometimes with a belt buckle."

More notes. "Do the beatings leave marks—scars or bruises?"

"Yes. Scars and bruises."

Notes. "Where do you sleep at night?"

"In the living room on the bed Uncle Issa and Aunt Sally bought me. Sometimes in the washroom in the back of the building when she throws me out of the apartment."

"Why does she throw you out of the apartment?"

"If I don't behave—you know, like not going to bed when I'm supposed to, or when I roughhouse."

"Does anyone ever touch you in your private places?"

I thought of the nice upstairs lady when I was four. "No."

Though I told the truth, I still felt conflicted. But I also knew that this was my chance to give information that would help me get to Sally and Issa. At one point, I also thought, *What the hell—why am I torn when she has no loyalty to me?*

I'm not sure how long the interview lasted, but it was simply the social services woman asking a question, my answer, her jotting notes, then another question. When I emerged from the office into the reception area, Mother looked stressed and calmly pissed. The red streaks on her arms—those that her blouse didn't cover—seemed redder.

"We'll be in touch" was all the interviewer said before she closed her door. I half hoped she'd send me to Sally and Issa right then and there. With the information I provided, how could she not?

"Let's go," was all Mother said. I suspect she knew I wouldn't lie for her. She'd come to expect that everyone in her life would betray her, so why should I be any different?

◆ ◆ ◆

On the bus home, Mother was more agitated than before.

She started to grill me about what happened the moment the bus pulled away from the curb. Her questions were specific: "What did she ask you? What did you say? How did she react?" I wanted to provide answers that would appease her without telling the full truth of what I was asked and what I said. If I tried to be vague, she became more agitated. "I want specifics, Mitchell," she'd say.

I escaped a beating that day, but Mother's behavior became more erratic. The restrictions on my behavior increased to the point where there was no more school or going outside on my own. I had no way to connect with Issa, and I imagined him patrolling the streets, worried and wondering what was happening with us.

Then Mother announced we were moving again.

"Where?" I asked. Regina, her eyes bright and wide, stood next to me.

It was not unusual that we were moving again. The last time I'd seen Issa, he told me to be hopeful, that the court would likely decide in our favor.

I was desperate to see Issa and thought, *I'm fucked. We're moving; the hearing's coming; how do I tell Sally and Issa?* Around this time, I remember looking up at the sky and envisioning that I was trapped in a big, bright cardboard box. "Here I am again . . ." I repeated quietly to myself.

Mother's scratching became worse as the move and court date neared. Using the tines of a fork to relieve the itching became her full-time preoccupation along with needing anything with citrus in it. She became weaker, though I would not describe her as weakened. One evening the upstairs neighbors had a party with loud music and dancing. The noise drove Mother wild to the point where she took a broom and banged it on the ceiling—*Boom! Boom! Boom!*—but to no effect. She became frantic. She threw the broom across the kitchen, opened the cupboards, and one by one, hurled our plates, bowls, glasses, anything she could get her hands on, up at the ceiling so the shards rained down around her. After about five minutes, she was exhausted and stopped. Breathless, she looked at me and said, "Well, now there'll be less for us to pack for our move." Then she laughed.

She's crazy, I thought, *but she has a hell of a sense of humor.*

◆ ◆ ◆

Our move was the day before the court hearing, and I worried Issa wouldn't be able to find me. That morning, Mother spoke to us in the voice of an excited child, "We're moving today! And this time we are going to fly on a plane! To a place that is very special and exciting!"

Fuck! How do I tell Issa? What's happening? What is she doing?

Our belongings were packed in large crates, which I thought was to make the job easier for the movers. Instead, they were packed so they could be shipped after we left. I had no idea where we were going. Mother still wouldn't tell me.

Soon after, Mother shooed us into a cab that took us to the airport.

"I don't want to go," I protested.

"Nonsense," Mother said. The scabs and bloody scratches on her legs and arms looked even more inflamed, and the whites of her eyes were a sallow yellow. "This will be fun. I promise." Then she pinched my arm hard enough to raise a welt and a bruise that turned a deep shade of purple.

The airport was a blur, as was getting on the plane, but I clearly remember sitting in an aisle seat. We first flew to New York City, where that evening we boarded another plane, the destination of which Mother had not shared. I sat alone next to a stranger with no idea where Mother and Regina were sitting. Not once during the ten-hour flight did Mother come to me to reassure me, much less tell me where we were going. It's hard even now to describe my loneliness and sense of isolation as I sat in the darkness of that plane.

It was still dark when I felt the wheels touch down, followed by the pilot announcing, "Welcome to Israel."

My heart sank. There would be no court, no more hope for a home with Issa and Sally. Everything was undone, dashed; the living hell would continue.

We walked from the terminal out into warm, dry night air, then to a bus stop. Mother was exhausted but led us like all this was nothing new, like it was another home to her—and it was. This was where my father came to find his bride while staying with his sister Ruska and her husband, Yosef, my aunt and uncle. Mother was that bride, but this story did not create any sensation of connection to a sense of help or hope.

Instead, Regina and I boarded the bus with Mother following behind. She had paused to pay the fare when her body buckled; she bent forward, grabbed her belly, and then collapsed. I rushed toward her, but she put her hand up, as if to say, "Give me a moment." The bus driver looked concerned, unsure of what to do. I stood a couple of feet from her, thinking, *This can't be happening. What's wrong with her? What's going to happen next?* I felt helpless and afraid in this foreign place at night, not knowing what was in store for us or what her plan was.

After several long moments, Mother regained her composure, paid the fare, then sat beside us. "It's nothing," she said. Neither Regina nor I had asked.

The world outside the bus was pitch black. We were the only people, and to my memory, it headed along a narrow country road, its headlights cutting through the darkness. The periphery of the light hinted at broad fields.

About an hour later we arrived in Yaffo (or Jaffa), a small coastal city south of Tel Aviv. Mother guided us to a hotel where we could hear gentle waves lapping at the beach just across the street. She checked us in. Her body showed the obvious signs of exhaustion and her illness. She'd brought a fork to continue her incessant scratching, but no one paid her much mind.

Keys in hand, we took the elevator to the third floor to what was a very sterile room with tile floors, white plaster walls, a cupboard, double bed, and coffee table.

"We're hungry," I complained to Mother. Regina nodded in agreement.

Exasperated, she said, "It's too late to eat now. Sleep."

The next morning Regina and I awoke to an entirely new world; the sounds of car horns, voices in odd languages, and buses came up through the lone window. We tried to rouse Mother, but she waved us off, too tired.

"But we're starving," we whined.

"Go away!" she responded, then rolled her body away from us.

We knew no one and didn't speak any Hebrew or Yiddish, but we had to at least take a peek at this new world, so we went down the elevator and emerged on a street that I would now describe as Old Israel. Loud diesel buses roared past, there were donkeys and horses—"Look! A horsey!" Regina called out—hauling flatbed carts loaded with produce and other items, cars speeding by using their horns as warnings to clear the way ahead of them, and, like a Middle Eastern bazaar, people, lots and lots of people: Jews of all descriptions, 1960s-era professionals, young hippy wanderers, attractive women and men, and Arabs of all descriptions moving to their own pace, in their own direction, for their own reasons, living their own lives amid a grand hustle and bustle. Across from this was a long, wide beach that swept down to deep blue water.

Standing just outside the foyer of the hotel felt like floating in a small eddy, a space to absorb that Mother had changed all of our lives by making this our new home.

Kitty-corner across the street was a *makolet*, a small, room-sized mom-and-pop grocery. The shelves were lined with canned goods, and there was some produce, cheeses, and meats. Behind the counter were rows of cigarettes, and a large rack held all sorts of candies, none of which we recognized. The owner asked us something, but we couldn't understand what he said.

We wandered for a while, our eyes wide with wonder and fear, but never going so far that we couldn't find our way back to the hotel and our mother. I convinced myself there was no way that Issa could find me. I felt completely disconnected from what I knew to be home, but also from any hope that this would be a temporary diversion from the path that led back to Sally and Issa. With each step and each new thing that I saw, it felt like I was moving further and further from the home and people I loved.

Hunger bit into our bellies, so we meandered back toward the hotel.

As we neared, a young woman in a business suit and carrying what looked like a leather messenger bag approached us.

"You must be Mitchell," she said.

I must have stuck out as an American kid: blond and dressed in black Converse sneakers, jeans, and a white t-shirt.

"I am," I replied.

"Hi, I'm here to help your mother and you and your sister . . ." She was a social worker.

For a moment, I thought this must mean Mother had been caught, that her abduction was known, and the authorities simply needed time to track us down to the correct city and hotel. It seemed miraculous that she appeared when she did. But now I realize she must have already set up an appointment with Mother.

"Your mother is not well," she said. "You and your sister are going to be placed in homes . . . We don't have room for you both in the same home . . . You'll be in a foster home . . . Your sister will be placed in Ben Shemen, an orphanage . . . Your mother is too ill . . . She has to go to hospital . . . We can't have you together . . ."

The memory of these words, each phrase landing in its own painful way, is of a steady stream as we stood in bright sun on a street corner in Yaffo, though in reality there was more than my memory presents.

"I'm sorry," she said. Her eyes winced just a little bit.

I can't imagine how Regina and I must have looked to her.

I picked up Regina's small hand, held it tight, and said, "Okay."

What more was there to say or do when you've lost everything and you're only ten years old?

Chapter 5

ADRIFT IN A
STRANGE LAND

I HATED SEPARATING FROM REGINA.

She was taken to a *kfar no'ar*—a type of boarding school developed in the 1930s to care for children and teens fleeing the Nazis—called Ben Shemen. Though it was and remains a beautiful campus of tan buildings with red-tiled roofs surrounded by palm and eucalyptus trees, to my seven-year-old sister, it was a strange place in a strange country. No one there knew who she was, and sadly, Regina had no one other than Mother and me to love her. With pain in their hearts, Sally and Issa would tell me, "She's not our family . . . She's not our blood," as a way of apologizing. As much as it hurt me to hear this, I did not and do not hold it against them. They had no legal right to her.

When we were separated, she couldn't have been more alone. That Regina could not speak Hebrew only added to her sense of isolation and uncertainty.

This was also when she and I started to become strangers to each other, living separated and separate lives.

I was taken to a modest second-floor duplex apartment in Netanya, a small city about a forty-minute drive north of Tel Aviv, to live with a family of two parents and three children: a fifteen-year-old girl, a boy my age, and a one-year-old boy. As with most foster care in the United States, the parents were paid to take in children in need of a stable home, and they were welcoming to me.

I arrived with the same suitcase I'd carried when I was first delivered to Mother and was given a bed in the same room as their older son. As with Regina at Ben Shemen, the family spoke Hebrew and knew only a little English. I knew no Hebrew at all, but with what little English they knew, they managed to convey that on the following Monday I would walk to school with their son. I had arrived at their home on the Sabbath (Friday) meaning there was no school or work that day.

That evening, we gathered around their small table—the toddler in his high chair—for dinner. They sat me at the head of the table opposite the father, which I took as a humbling gesture of kindness. The mother prepared and served the meal and then poured each of us a glass of orange soda that was popular throughout Israel. We started to eat, the table was quiet, and I gulped down the soda, which was a rare treat for me and the first such thing I'd had since we'd left Los Angeles.

I held my glass out toward the mother. "May I have some more?"

Each eye at the table stared at me as if I'd said I would now like to fly around the room. Embarrassment warmed my face.

"Welcoming the stranger" is a core tradition and cultural norm within the Jewish community, even more so in Israel, a country composed of so many immigrants. It is in part based on the credo *tikkun olam*, which loosely means "repairing the world." The father looked at the mother; the mother looked at the father. The children looked at the parents and at one another as if I'd breached some set protocol. Their eyes and expressions seemed to say, "He's a guest in our home, the proverbial stranger. What do we do now?"

The mother looked at me. "Of course."

As soon as she'd filled my glass, the other kids held theirs out, too, and she refilled each one. Unwittingly, I'd just changed a family norm; from then on, it was "yes, more soda if you would like."

The next day, Sunday, their daughter put a small 45-rpm record on the turntable and turned the volume up. The voice was unmistakably Elvis and the song "Jailhouse Rock." From the first note, we started jumping around the living room, bouncing off one another, and at times slipping into Elvis-hip-shaking impressions. This would be the first of thousands of times we would play this one song. I still have no idea what the B-side song on that record was.

◆ ◆ ◆

Monday morning came, and with it the call to wake by the mother. Her son and I rose, performed our morning ablutions, then ate breakfast. I sat quietly eating within a whorl of incomprehensible Hebrew and frenetic family activity. The father drove a delivery truck and rushed about to prepare for his day. The mother was the keeper of the home, a true *balabusta*. She was busy caring for the diapered youngest son while preparing breakfast and lunches for her husband, kids, and me.

And then she shooed us all from the house.

The son and I walked a few blocks to a small cement school. As I think of the building today, it reminds me of a charter or Montessori school. The son guided me to the principal, who was ready for me to arrive. He spoke some English but mostly Hebrew, and quickly. He ushered me down a hallway to a classroom, then opened the door and gestured for me to enter. A few words were spoken to the teacher, and she guided me to a desk.

For the next few hours, I understood little to nothing of what was said. Meanwhile, the other kids stared at me—the weirdly dressed, obviously American kid whose expression maintained a constant state of dumbfounded befuddlement. Math was at least known to me; numbers are numbers. Every so often, one of the kids would ask in broken English, "Do you have the time?" or "What's your name?" They wore watches on their wrists, so I had no idea what the point of the questions were or why they seemed so fixated on knowing the time. Later, I figured out that in their English class they'd just learned about how to ask what the time is.

Lunch break came, and with it a sense that I could breathe again. I stood against an outside wall watching the other boys eat, then play soccer. *Boy, do I stand out like a sore thumb*, I thought. I wanted to disappear and wasn't sure if I wanted anyone to even speak to me.

That night I lay in bed thinking long and hard about the next morning. Now as an adult, when I think of my education, I can't help but repeat the line in *On the Waterfront* by Marlon Brando, "I coulda been a contendah." I love psychology. I love law. I love anatomy. I love to be curious, to learn, and if things had been different, I might have had a chance to follow these pathways. But in the earliest grades, the most oft-heard teacher comment was, "He's always daydreaming... He's not here." When one thinks of the effects of trauma on a child's mind, one thinks of dissociation, which includes the ability—voluntary or involuntary—to escape physical and emotional pain through disappearing within the mind. That was me as a child. Even before leaving for Israel, I'd been held back two grades in school. I felt stupid and unredeemable as a student. When in fact, I was just a kid trying to survive my mother.

I was robbed of my abilities, of a possible future.

That I believed I was a terrible student—stupid—helped ease what I would do the next morning.

"I'm not going," I said amid the maelstrom of the family's preparations for the day.

"What?" the mother asked.

"I'm not going back to school," I said.

The mother knew enough English for us to hold an awkward and hesitating conversation.

"But you must," she said, shocked that I could make such a choice.

"But this is stupid. I have no idea what they are talking about."

Again, our language barrier made true communication nearly impossible. I understood the meaning of most of her words more through divining her facial expressions and the tone of her body. Clearly, she was upset but unsure.

To help us, she called over a neighbor who spoke English. He was in his early twenties and recently discharged from the IDF (Israeli Defense Forces). Service is a universal requirement of citizens, and he was considering what to do with his life now that he was free of that obligation.

Through this interpreter she explained, "I don't know what it is like in the United States, but in Israel, you must go to school."

"Why am I being subjected to this?" I asked, my voice rising with anger. "It's bad enough what my mom did, but now I'm in a classroom where I have no idea what is being said or taught. It's stupid, and I'm not going."

Through the neighbor, the mother pushed back some, but I suppose she could clearly read my tone, expression, and body language. Also, when I said my mom was bad enough, she seemed to hear that in a way that only a mother who truly loves her children would. She knew I wasn't here—her house, Israel, anywhere—by my own choice. I think, too, that her fostering experiences taught her to stand firm but be flexible when necessary.

I looked at the mother. "No school! No more!"

"Okay," she said in English. And that was it. No more school.

From here, life fell into a new regular, if not relatively boring, routine of walking around the neighborhood, spending some time with the English-speaking neighbor, and then playing with the son when he came home from school.

After a month, things began to get sticky with the son. When I first arrived, we got along well. He was more than happy to have a boy his age to pal around and play with, even if language was a barrier. But after I quit school, resentments began to build. Me not going to school was part of it, as was some of the attention I received from the mother. She wanted me to feel comfortable and probably had a sense of what my life had been like with Mother, so I got a little extra or softer attention. Her son probably also resented having to share his space and belongings on top of sharing his parents.

We started to bicker, then argue, and eventually we came close to blows. The parents were torn. They wanted to support their son, but they understood my situation, that it was temporary, and they wanted to foster more children as a *mitzvah*—good deed in the eyes of God—and for the income.

Their son wasn't torn. He wanted me out of his room and his house.

About six weeks after I'd arrived, the same social worker returned to the house.

"How's life here?" she asked.

"It's okay," I said.

"Just okay?" She sensed the hesitancy in my voice.

"I'm not getting along with their son like I used to," I said. "I don't really like it here."

"How do the parents treat you?" she asked. "Do you feel they want you here?"

"They are fine to me, but they love their son." I looked up at her. "I don't want to stay here anymore. I don't like it here."

She nodded. "Your mother's still very ill, too ill to take care of you yet, but she misses you and wanted me to tell you she'll see you soon hopefully."

I nodded. I really didn't care if I ever saw her again.

She leaned a little closer. "There's space for you at Ben Shemen, where Regina is."

I looked up. I missed Regina so much.

"There are lots of children there, it's a good place, and you would be with your sister again. Would you like to live there?"

"Yes, very much. Yes, please," I said.

The social worker spoke with the mother, but I don't think she accurately explained how I was feeling. I didn't want her or the father to feel hurt or take any blame for how I felt. They'd done all they could.

But the mother looked at me. "I don't understand. You aren't happy here?" she asked in broken English.

With the help of the social worker, I tried to explain to this surrogate mother that I was unhappy, but it was nothing against her. Yet again I was trying to comfort a parent in a strange predicament not of my own making. I didn't want her to feel hurt, and here she was feeling very hurt. But this was my opportunity to leave, to be with Regina.

She said she understood, but deep worry was still written across her eyes, caught in the tone of her voice. It remained that way for the next week, until the social worker returned, and with my little suitcase, she took me to Ben Shemen.

◆ ◆ ◆

If life with Mother and then the foster family was a desert, Ben Shemen was an oasis. Lots of kids, wide yards shaded by palm and eucalyptus trees, a community swimming pool, a working farm and dairy, and a predictable, stable schedule and life.

And as one would expect with so many, there was also plenty of mischief to be had. The dairy comprised wide open fields for the cows to graze, a large barn where they were housed, and a milking parlor with cooled storage, a pasteurization system, and an office. All of it was

off-limits. As if that wasn't seduction enough for kids, the dairy manager
was a mean old crank. Word had it that if he caught you trying to climb
the fence or you were generally anywhere you weren't supposed to be,
he'd grab you by the cuff and smear you in cow shit.

Sneaking into the dairy—barn, field, parlor—was considered a test
of one's courage and ability to outrace the manager. My friends and I
loved it.

My one disappointment was not seeing Regina as much as I wanted
or, truthfully, needed. The boys lived in one dorm, the girls another, and
largely led separate lives. Though we would sneak into the dairy, slipping
into the girls' dorm was a whole other matter.

"Where's Malka's brother?" four girls yelled as they burst into the
boys' wing a week or so after I arrived.

Regina was now going by her Hebrew name, Malka.

"Over there," said a boy, pointing at me.

They rushed toward me, shouting in broken English over one another
to be heard, "Malka no see!" . . . "She need you!" . . . "Very bad!"

As a quartet, they pointed down the corridor. Five girls were leading
Malka down the corridor toward me, with Malka crying, "I'm blind! I'm
blind! I can't see! It stings, Mitchell!"

I ran toward her. "You're not blind! You're not blind! I'm here. I'll
take care of you!"

When I got to her, I could see that a thick crud had built up along the
seam of her eyelashes and eyelids as if they were glued shut.

"I don't believe you!" Malka sobbed as if she were releasing the past
two months of loneliness, loss, and pain.

"It's true," I said. "Here, come here," and I led her to a sink where I
started to splash water on her eyes.

At first, it didn't help, and Malka cried harder, her panic edging
higher, her breathing fast and shallow.

"More water . . . It'll work . . . Stop crying!" I said.

After a few moments of what seemed like an eternity to us, the water started to thin the crust, and she could begin to open her eyes. More scrubbing and washing got rid of the gunk, her breathing and crying eased, and she seemed to return to normal.

Malka wasn't the only child to "go blind" that day, so the pool was closed. After a few days, the adults realized that a new chemical treating the pool water was the cause. Poor Malka had gone for a swim and then took a nap. When she woke up, she couldn't see, and every emotion buried within her came pouring out.

◆ ◆ ◆

In Israel, the Sabbath begins at sunset on Friday. It's a day set aside to God, a day of rest and no work, including chores such as cleaning and cooking, or even driving. For many, Friday is either a day off from work—the equivalent of Saturday in the United States—or a half-day of work, and Friday evening includes the lighting of candles, prayer, and a meal with friends and family.

So, when a social worker approached me one Thursday, I had only anticipated playing with friends.

She smiled. "Mitchell, your mother would like to see you." Her eyes widened. "Isn't that wonderful?"

"No. I don't want to see *her*."

Her smile ebbed. "But Mitchell, you and Malka can go to her, be with her for a little bit today. She misses you very much."

My eyes wandered from hers. "I don't miss her."

"But she loves you very much."

"If you knew what she's been doing to me, you wouldn't say that."

She placed her hands on her hips. "Mitchell, she's your mother, and you only have one mother."

She may have meant well, but she was telling me that I should love my abuser, the person who made my life a living hell.

"You don't understand; she's a horrible person."

She pressed her lips together for a beat. "She's *your* mother, and *she* wants to see you."

"No."

Her head tilted forward. "Your mother wants to see you."

"No."

Of all the Israeli social workers Malka and I met, this woman would not be deterred, no matter how many times I said no. I finally gave in when I realized I was moments away from being hauled by the scruff into the parking lot and shoved into her car.

◆ ◆ ◆

I was surprised by the tranquility of Mother's convalescent hospital.

It looked like an old British military hospital, something you'd see in the movies. It was probably built during World War I and comprised long, wide buildings like large bungalows that surrounded a grassy quadrangle. The front of each building was landscaped with flower gardens shaded by palm and eucalyptus trees with fat, round trunks. Walkways led across the quadrangle to the doorway of each building, and another walkway ran around the perimeter. Within the grassy area, there were little copses of two or three trees with a bench or table and chairs set beneath the shade.

A nurse led Malka, the social worker, and me to one of these shaded tables.

"Your mother knows you are here, so wait here, please," the nurse said, then walked off.

I gave the social worker a hard look. "Let's just get this over with."

She gave me a harder look.

Malka was wiggly in her chair. "Mitchell," she said. Her voice was soft, a mild rebuke for peace.

The calm beauty surrounding us belied my deep agitation. "I just want to get back home."

"We will soon," scolded the social worker.

We sat for about twenty minutes without saying a word. The same nurse that showed us in returned. "Your mother's quite weak today and having a bit of a slow start—"

Why am I here? I thought. *Something's not right.*

"—She'll be out in a few minutes."

A few minutes later Mother emerged from a bungalow door wearing a blue hospital gown. Her steps were timid, shaky. A male nurse had her arm, helping her. They made it down a short walkway, then onto the grass near a stand of three palms. She hesitated, placed her free hand on the palm, leaned her head down, and retched.

The nurse turned Mother around and guided her back to the door.

The social worker shifted in her seat. "Your mother is not feeling well. She needs to go back to her room."

And that was it. Reunion over.

I didn't know it then, but Mother had had one or two major surgeries. She would never get better, and for the next twenty years, her body would slowly decay until she died. A slow death and a horrible life. As a child, her parents divorced, then the Nazis invaded her home in Poland. She watched her mother die on a lousy table while hiding in a barn, followed by loneliness, confined spaces, and knowing every second of every day that the Nazis were looking to kill her and the people hiding her could turn on her at any moment. Afterward, as a teenager, she fled Soviet occupation to Canada where she married for the first time, divorced, fled to Israel, then joined the IDF, but was soon kicked out. She married again, moved to the United States, divorced once more, gave me up to an orphanage, took me back, beat me incessantly, then kidnapped me to Israel. And on and on.

Her actions were reckless and selfish, and while I have sympathy for the life she lived and how she was a product of what happened to her as a girl, I don't excuse how she treated me or Malka. She tore me from Sally and Issa to live within her chaotic, angry, and violent grasp.

The last time I saw my mother before she died, she committed one final, indecent act of betrayal.

But that was twenty years away from the day Malka and I watched her vomit against a palm tree. The pathetic ugliness of that has never left my memory, nor has Malka's expression of pain, despair, and fear.

I have nothing but love and sadness for Malka. Such a sweet girl to have such a hard life.

And if not for her crayon scribbling before we left Los Angeles, I may never have found my way home.

Chapter 6

ALIYAH

ALIYAH IS AN IMPORTANT concept in Judaism.

It's a Hebrew word that translates as "the act of going up, elevation," or "ascension." To Israelis, it holds three usages. The first is to describe the honor of the rabbi calling a worshipper to the *Bimah*—an elevated platform at the center of a synagogue—to read a selection from the Torah.

The second—often termed "making an Aliyah"—is the act of Jews immigrating or returning to Israel. It is foundational to the Law of Return that enshrines the right of all Jews to make an Aliyah.

The third refers to a set of government-provided services managed by the Ministry of Aliyah to assist those making an Aliyah with housing, employment, healthcare, and cultural integration.

For children making an Aliyah like Malka (seven) and me (ten), Ben Shemen was a government service sponsored by the Ministry of Aliyah. It was also a center for Jews from all over the world to volunteer as a *mitzvah*—an altruistic religious duty—in service to Judaism.

Within this context, Malka and I were thought of and treated as two children making an Aliyah with their sickened mother. There were promises by social workers and others that she loved and missed us and we would soon be returned to her once she'd recovered.

The conviction of the adults and volunteers that we were on a type of Judaic pilgrimage, soon to be returned to our loving mother (i.e., abuser), cemented my sense of dislocation and despair. It exacerbated my intensely deep fears that Issa, Sally, and my father either couldn't find me or, painfully, had given up. By this point, we had been in Israel for nearly six months. How could I think otherwise?

When a young volunteer with an accent I did not recognize asked me to follow her to the central office because I had a visitor, I assumed it was another social worker. At best, a social worker was checking in to see how I was doing. At worst, it would be the news that Mother had recovered and we would be leaving Ben Shemen—a place of relative happiness—to reunite with her.

We walked outdoors along a well-worn pathway around the corner of the administration building to emerge into a courtyard that spread out from the building's entrance.

"Mitchell! We've been looking for you for so long!"

"Issa!" I cried as I ran into his arms. Not usually a physically affectionate person, he held me tight. I didn't want to let go.

I stepped back, he tussled my hair, a wide, wide smile spread across his lips. "We've missed you so very much."

"I've missed you, too."

His smile broadened. "Mitchell, we didn't know where you went, where you were."

"I know, I know," I said, my eyes wandered from his. "I'm sorry. I had no way to tell you."

His smile ebbed. "It's okay, Mitchell, it's okay. You did leave us a message. We were able to get into your mother's apartment to look around, and we saw scribbled in crayon on the floor, 'We are moving to New York.'"

I laughed and said, "That was Regina!"

He laughed, too. "So, I hired a private investigator to find you . . ."

For me? I thought.

Issa told me that they didn't find a hint of us in New York, which got Issa, Sally, and Dad to consider that Mother was using her maiden name. This then led them to think that Dad had met Mother in Israel where she had a deep connection—she'd been kicked out of the IDF—so they searched Israel using her maiden name. Helping them in Israel was my Uncle Shraga—the brother of my Aunt Ruska, a woman I'd never met and knew little of who had played the role of matchmaker for my parents. Shraga was an educated and intellectual man who'd made and nurtured solid connections within the Israeli government, which he used to track me down at Ben Shemen.

For me? I thought again.

"We're working with Shraga to get you back, to bring you home. It won't happen overnight—it will take time—but we're doing all we can. Sally and I want you to live with us again. Your father wants that, too."

Pure joy. That was how it felt to see this man and hear these words. Absolute honesty. Absolute integrity and honor. Unconditional love.

"What about Malka?" I asked.

"Malka?"

I explained her name change and that it meant "queen" in Hebrew.

"She deserves such a name," Issa said, "but there isn't anything we can do for her. We have no legal right unless her father were to agree to something, but no one knows who he is."

I wanted to be home with Issa so much that I would accept nothing less, but the seed of guilt took root when Malka and I were separated.

By now, boys surrounded Issa and me, most of them friends, enticed by this wonderous miracle of a parent or relative come to bring one of us home. They were wide-eyed at this show of love, respect, and possibility.

"Come with me, Issa. I want to show you my room."

We started walking to my dorm followed by the passel of boys, most of whom spoke little English. My Hebrew was passable.

"Holy fuck!" one of them said.

Issa kept walking, like he'd not heard.

"Shit, how the fuck you?" another asked.

My face burned. Issa kept walking as if he heard none of it. Not even an eyebrow raised.

"You fucking shit good man!" the smallest boy announced.

Like the kids at my previous school, these kids were learning English and liked to practice on me. To my eternal shame and embarrassment, I had taught them a little too much.

When we got to the dorm, I showed Issa where I lived. Then back outside, the boys and I went back to playing tag. Issa watched; his smile broad, loving, proud.

◆ ◆ ◆

Issa stayed in Israel for a couple of weeks, even bringing me to Haifa to meet my Aunt Ruska, her husband, Yosef, and Uncle Shraga. Yosef and Ruska lived in a modest one-bedroom apartment on the top floor of a three-story building. Shraga—never married and no taller than four and a half feet who walked with a limp—lived in a small studio down the street.

Theirs was a modest home and life, but in the brief couple of hours I spent with them, it was obvious that these people were filled with love and laughter—and so much food. "Eat, eat," Ruska admonished. "He looks like a waif!" she said to Issa.

Perhaps there were tough times that at ten years old I couldn't detect, but I was enthralled by these people. That I was so closely related to them—Ruska and Shraga were my father's brother and sister!—made me feel connected to a broader family, a broader history, a larger identity.

When Issa said it was time to bring me back to Ben Shemen, it was hard to leave.

A week or so later, it was time for Issa to leave, and he came to Ben Shemen to say goodbye. Before he left, he promised that Shraga was leaning on his contacts to get a court hearing for me. The effort that began in Los Angeles would continue in Israel. Of course, I believed him and held out hope, but I'd learned that hope is sometimes a fiction.

"Hang in there, Mitchell. We're doing all we can," he said. "I'll be back soon."

I watched him walk out the doorway of Ben Shemen like the free man he was. I was still captive, not too unhappily as this was infinitely better than life with Mother, but a captive, nonetheless.

◆ ◆ ◆

About a month later, a young woman came up to me. "There's someone at the central office to see you."

I followed her, this time with the thought that perhaps this would be the news I had long waited for, the words that would free me.

Instead, it was a social worker.

"Mitchell, good news," she said brightly. My anticipation grew. "Your mother is well enough for you to live with her again."

Is this really happening? I thought.

My eyes, my expression, my whole body drooped. I was shocked and disappointed by this news and wondered what was next for Malka and me.

The Ministry of Aliyah provided us with a small income and apartment in Kiryat Haim, a seaside suburb north of Haifa composed of humble homes and apartment buildings. Ours was a modest two-bedroom, one-bath unit on the second floor of a four-story building that stood as one in a row like dominoes leading to the beach. Between each was a dirt-and-grass courtyard where we played with the many other kids living in these buildings. Like ours, their families were of limited means, many of them refugees making an Aliyah—quite a few were Russian—the remainder the dispossessed of Israel. There was a sadness and hopelessness to the buildings and people that contrasted with the beauty of the nearby beaches.

Despite each social worker promising Mother's recovery, she was gravely ill. Her skin was jaundiced, the whites of her eyes a sickly yellow. Scabs ran up and down her legs and arms from the continued use of anything sharp—usually forks—to scratch the sores that itched interminably. Her energy level was low, her temper high. She was too ill to beat me as she used to, but this did not stop her from hitting me if I came too close or pinching my skin with her unusually strong yet cadaverous fingers.

Mother's public behavior, never great, deteriorated. I remember standing in line at the pharmacy with her (that she had the energy to go to the pharmacy was unusual). A young woman in her late teens with long, full red hair—a *gingy* in Israel—stood in front of us. Mother touched her hair with her hand, wiping it down as if petting a horse's mane, saying in her weakened voice, "Look at how pretty is her hair."

The young woman turned and looked at Mother but said nothing. I imagine she considered the yellow, scab-covered woman touching her hair and thought better of saying anything.

A public nurse—like one from a visiting nurse association in the United States—came once each week to check on Mother and give her some kind of shot to help her itching. It didn't do much or last too long. It was like putting a Band-Aid on a gunshot wound. Mother would give me short grocery lists to take to the *makolet* (market). She craved citrus, especially concentrated grapefruit or lemon juices that were supposed to be thinned with water but that she drank straight from the bottle. This was yet another sign of the damage to her liver, which caused me to wonder if she was dying and question her discharge from the convalescent hospital. *Why would they do this to us?* I often wondered.

These little groceries were all the food we had to eat. True to his word, Issa did come back to Israel a couple of months after Malka and I moved back in with Mother. He picked me up—as tense a moment as one could expect—and took me to Yosef and Ruska's where Shraga arrived to visit with us. Shraga and Issa shared a hushed conversation then sat down to a meal with family. It was as lovely as my first experience with these members of my extended family. This time the small apartment and table was filled with cousins—including Ruska and Yosef's two older sons, both married, and eighteen-year-old daughter, about to get married, and friends. All the while Ruska encouraged me to eat, and Yosef was not shy about tousling my hair; a few times he even interrupted the conversation—more a melee of voices—to say, "Please, I want to share this with Mitchell . . ." and then spoke to me as if I were his honored guest. When he did this, I felt respected and loved.

If Yosef started to get too excited, Ruska interrupted, "Yosef, your heart." Each time she did this, she'd look at me. "Mitchell, Uncle Yosef has a bad heart; we have to protect him—never let him get angry, too excited, or . . ." Then her voice would fade. It was surprising to me that such a happy, gregarious man with what seemed like a limitless number of stories to tell could have such a weak heart.

After the meal, Yosef pulled Issa aside to tell him that he and Ruska were worried that I was eating enough. Issa thought I looked wan and knew our past issues with food insecurity. He agreed to set up a credit account at the small makolet for me to use for Malka and me and pay the bill. After he left a week or so later, I was too shy to use it. The elderly couple who owned the makolet sneered at me, which made me believe they were unkind and judgmental. I may have misread their sneers as judgment of our financial straits when it was more likely because I was obviously American. At the time, if you wore tennis shoes—as I always did—Israelis instantly knew you were American. Everyone else—adults, kids, immigrants, rich, poor— wore sandals. After my sneakers wore out, so did I. In the end, I only used the account a few times for a small amount of candy.

◆ ◆ ◆

Issa had told me to remain hopeful, that Mother had kidnapped me, which meant the current situation would not last forever. But it was now months since Malka and I had left Ben Shemen. I started to truly believe that hope was a fiction, a story of a day that would never come.

Mother was angry and hateful. The world owed her, wasn't paying up—it was even out to get her—and she took this out on me. Malka lived a life of quiet isolation. Mother never hit her and rarely yelled at her. Malka was a sweet, wide-eyed child. Ben Shemen was nothing more than a break from life with Mother. I would never be free; this would last forever.

I was also watching Mother die. Even to me—eleven years old now— it was clear she was dying. If she'd ever had anything worth losing other than her life, I'd say she was Job lying in dust and ashes covered in boils. But of course, Job repented. That wasn't Mother's style. On a good day, she had the strength to get up, but a normal day was her lying in the apartment scratching at her skin with a fork, scabs and blood running down her arms and legs, forehead and abdomen. Always itching, itching, itching, getting thinner . . . becoming ever more jaundiced. Then a shot, a brief reprieve, but soon back to the dust and ashes—unrepentant, unloving, unlovable.

◆ ◆ ◆

It was late afternoon Friday. By sundown, nearly all of Israel would shut down for the Sabbath. Mother was irritated and lying in her bed in the living room. Our little kitchen nook with a table and three chairs was just behind her.

I noticed her purse laying open on the table, the corner of a five-lira note peeking out from the lip of the purse like a little tongue. She'd just yelled at me and pinched me. A welt was forming, and I was angry. I looked at Mother—as she scratched herself with a fork—then back to her purse and the corner of the five-lira note. Malka was in her room playing—a version of hiding, escapism.

Fighting back was useless. I remained quiet. Malka, like she had some radar for Mother's moods, ceased verbalizing her imaginary play.

I'm leaving, I thought.

◆ ◆ ◆

Once when I was nine and we still lived in Los Angeles, I had taken a dollar bill from Mother's purse. For too many days and weeks, I'd heard the tinny music of the ice-cream truck, unable to buy anything. I'd watched other kids line up, most with ten or twenty cents, the going rate for most of the treats.

With the dollar in my hand, I ran outside to where the ice-cream truck was parked, my conscience pricked by my theft but intent on being like the other kids. I'd never bought ice cream from the old, rough-looking man who drove the truck. I stood in line watching his every move; he reminded me of Popeye the Sailor Man. Take an order, turn to the little freezer cabinets, withdraw a treat, receive the dime or twenty cents, hand over the ice cream or frozen pop or whatever, and then, if he had to make change, use his thumb to work the levers on the silver four-barrel changemaker hanging from his belt.

I was last in line, and I worried that I had too much money, that I'd have jangling change that could give away my theft to Mother. Where could I hide the change when I had no privacy? I decided that I'd order the most expensive thing.

The man reached into the small freezer, withdrew the ice cream, and handed it to me. I handed over the dollar bill, and he worked the changemaker with his thumb. In quick succession, a small pile of dimes dropped into his hand. Panic sparked from the sight of all those coins. I turned and ran as fast as I could.

"Hey! Where are you goin'?" he called out. "Your change!"

He leapt from his truck and chased after me. I tripped and fell in the grass on someone's front lawn. He grabbed my hand and placed the change in it. "Here's your change, you crazy kid."

Terrified, I ran into an alley that I knew would be the quickest path home. Along the way, I tossed the coins and the treat into some ivy. I raced back home and burst through the front door. Mother looked up at me. My eyes veered from hers. The tinny music of the ice-cream truck neared our home as a slow-motion doppler effect. I became deeply afraid that he would stop in front of our apartment, leave his truck, and express his suspicions of me to Mother. I peeked out the window, praying he would just keep going. Thank God. He did.

I turned to see Mother staring at me as if I'd lost my mind.

◆ ◆ ◆

To steal the five-lira note, I risked Mother seeing me from her periphery, but I quietly slipped into the kitchen nook, slid the five-lira note from the mouth of her purse, and pushed it into my pocket.

I felt worse in this moment than I had stealing the dollar, but not enough to put the money back. *I'll repay her, one day*, I promised myself.

As I passed Mother, I said, "Going out. Going to play."

She waved her hand as permission.

I walked from the room out into the hallway. I closed the door softly, like I didn't want to wake a sleeping baby. I ran down the stairs to the landing, then to the bus stop as if Mother was in the bloom of youth, her health restored, fierce and on my tail.

At the bus stop, breathless, I looked down the street, but there wasn't a bus coming. *Come on, come on, where are you?* I thought, feeling like the escapee I was.

The bus arrived; I climbed on, handed over the five lira, received change, then found a seat toward the back. The second I heard the doors close, the diesel engine rise, and the bus ease forward away from the curb, I let out a long, deep breath. On the next inhale, the full force of guilt passed through me like an electrical current. I had stolen money, I was leaving Mother . . . and worse, Malka was still quietly playing in her room, unaware that once again, beyond her control, her life had changed.

My thin, undernourished body could not release the accumulated tension. I got off at what I hoped was the right stop.

Thank God, it was. I ran to Ruska and Yosef's building, my sandals slapping at each of the marble steps as I raced up. At the door, I rang the bell.

"Mitchell?" Ruska said when she opened the door wearing her apron.

"I ran away."

She looked at me for a moment as if to size up the situation. "Mitchell, come in," she said, her voice warm.

Yosef came to me, tousled my hair. "Welcome, Mitchell, welcome." He gave a worried look to Ruska that said, *What do we do now?*

"We have to call Sally and Issa," Ruska said.

I had no idea what Issa and Sally would say. They might feel this was a step too far, that I'd compromised their carefully laid legal plan. In fact, I believed this to probably be the "responsible" response.

Ruska dialed the number, sending an impulse thousands of miles away. The staticky hello, an explanation, Ruska—with Yosef leaning close to the receiver—asked, "What should we do?"

Issa's voice leaked from her ear, "Keep him."

"Keep him?"

"Yes. Keep him."

Ruska hung up. Looked at Yosef. Yosef nodded.

"You can stay," she said, "but we must inform your mother."

Shit!

Chapter 7

"MITCHELL, THE MOST AMAZING THING HAPPENED..."

RUSKA MADE UP THE PULLOUT COUCH as a bed for me in their sitting room while I sat in the kitchen with Yosef. "Mitchell," he said, "I had the most wonderful conversation with Issa about you. Let me tell you about it . . ."

He said how much Issa and Sally loved me, that they wanted nothing more in life than for me to be home with them, that I must be a special person to have earned so much of their love. The way he spoke was quiet, reverential, but with the smile of a man who took joy in saying such things to me.

Ruska and Yosef said goodnight and turned out the light. I lay in the darkness, a streetlight illuminating the small room. There was a coffee table Ruska had moved to make room for the bed, a TV, and photos of family hanging or standing in every available space. Off the sitting room was a balcony with louvered shades letting light in from the street.

That I was here seemed unreal in a fantastical sort of way. A thought of Malka pricked my conscience, but I was too sleepy for it to cause much of a rise; then I drifted off.

The next morning, I awoke to a cacophony of cars, diesel buses, and trucks roaring up and down Pinat Herzl, a congested and noisy boulevard with the exhaust of so many vehicles floating over it. The tenor of truck and bus engines rose to climb the steep hill by the apartment or groaned against the gears and brakes as they descended. A chorus of voices slipped through the louvres making for a mental image of chaotic but intentional hustle and bustle on the boulevard below. The outside world was alive, and its noise bounced off the walls in the apartment.

My thoughts were captured by the sound of it. As much as I missed Los Angeles, Israel was exerting a certain pull on me.

In an instant, though, my escape from Mother rushed into my mind as an intrusive thought. An image of Malka waking up alone yet again pained my stomach. Despite Mother's illness, she could come snatch me any moment or somehow ambush me. With this thought, the sensation of being a prey animal constantly wary of its surroundings and threats became an almost permanent way of being.

◆ ◆ ◆

Over the next days and weeks, as Shraga pressed his contacts and worked my case through the government and Israeli legal system, I came to know Yosef and Ruska as two of the happiest people I'd ever met. Yosef—retired with a pension from the electric utility—was truly a joyous person whose smile was nearly constant. He loved to tell me stories that often started with, "Mitchell, the most interesting thing happened . . ." or "Mitchell, I want to share this conversation with you . . ." or "I had the funniest thing happen, let me tell you, Mitchell . . ." He made me feel that sharing each conversation, event, or humorous anecdote with me gave him particular joy. If the two of us went out together, say to the post office or on some errand, we usually ran into friends of his or witnessed some event that caused him to smile, leading to a new story. We'd walk through the door, and he'd immediately say to Ruska or anyone else who happened to be in their home, "Mitchell and I had the most amazing thing happen . . ." or "Mitchell said something that was so funny/interesting, let me tell you about it . . ." He loved bringing these stories home, and because he included me in his caring, exceptional way, I felt valued, maybe even a little special.

Most afternoons, he'd take a little siesta-like rest in his and Ruska's bedroom where he'd lie back with his shirt off, exposing his broad, hairy chest. I'd sometimes wander in to tease him. "Gorilla chest," I'd say, and with his eyes gently closed, he'd smile, and then, more often than not, tell me yet another story.

His nature was always toward happiness, and to my knowledge, his only nemesis was his heart. "Don't let him get upset . . . Don't let him get emotional . . . Don't let him get *verklempt* . . . His sick heart can't take it . . . You'll make sure, right, Mitchell?" Ruska often said to me. If Yosef were to get angry or overexcited, Ruska was there to admonish, "Your heart, your heart, *yakiri*. Calm down!"

Often, Yosef would laugh and say, "I'm fine, *yakira*." Then he'd look at me, holding his hand in front of him. "See, Mitchell? Steady. I'm good."

Ruska was the happy, loving, slightly anxious *balabusta* of the home. To her, cooking was an act of love. *Salat katzutz*, a staple of most Israeli tables, is a mix of chopped cucumbers, onions, and tomatoes seasoned with olive oil, lemon juice, salt, and pepper. Ruska used an inexpensive and fairly common plastic handled paring knife to cube the vegetables over a large bowl. No cutting board, just the vegetables dropping almost perfectly from her hand. My favorite was *salat katzutz* with boiled chicken feet, which to any American sounds terrible, but in her capable hands was a special treat with an incredible texture. She always shopped at the same butcher and would announce with no small hint of pride that she'd prepared the chicken feet "especially for Mitchell."

With each other, Ruska and Yosef were profoundly affectionate without the affection of touch, at least not in front of anyone else. It was in the way they looked and smiled at each other, their gentle and loving way of speaking to each other. Physical intimacy, even a kiss or holding hands, was a personal thing between them to be shared privately. For me, there was an enduring beauty to their way of being.

They were very much in love and made me feel loved, deeply loved, even as my sense of hypervigilance—a PTSD reward from Mother's abuse—meant that I never truly felt safe. Whenever the phone rang or there was a knock at the door, my heart raced at the thought that it was Mother with the police.

A few days after I arrived, Ruska and Yosef decided, with my wary agreement, that I should return to school. Because it was the middle of the winter term, it would be too difficult to enter a new school near Pinat Herzl. So, I returned to the school near Mother's apartment. Each day that I walked past the building where Mother and Malka lived, I held my breath, expecting that from any corner, at any moment, Mother would seize me. Lending additional urgency to my fear was the guilt I felt over Malka. I'd left her, knowing she'd have to endure our angry, slowly dying mother alone.

In the end, Malka was removed from Mother's care. This was three or four weeks after I ran off. I learned at school that she'd been taken away, but no one could tell me where. When I told Ruska and Yosef, they asked Shraga to look into it, which was how I came to find that Malka was sent to an orphanage similar to Ben Shemen in Kiryat Bialik, a few miles north of Haifa. It was called Ahava, the Hebrew word for "love."

A month or so later, I went alone to Ahava to visit Malka. Though it was similar in its function to Ben Shemen, it lacked the beautiful grounds and trees and yards of Ben Shemen. Instead, it was a collection of buildings that I wandered around, asking whomever I met, "Do you know Malka? Where is she?" Little by little I zeroed in on her until I finally found her.

She approached me, then stopped. Her eight-year-old eyes stared at me, impassive, tinged by sadness, anger. "You left me," she said.

I hadn't known what to expect. Anger was a possibility, but I'd hoped for something else. Perhaps relief that we'd both made it out. But of course, I'd found a family and loving home with the hope of returning to Sally and Issa. Malka was back to a type of incarceration where she was one child of many needing a type of love that no institution can provide.

We were in two different worlds. Abruptly, things had changed when I ran away.

"I'm sorry," I said.

She rocked from heel to toe for a moment. "I don't like it here. I'm glad I'm away from Mother, but I don't like it here."

"What happened?" I asked.

"Mother was too ill to take care of me. That's what the nurse said, and they came and took me here." She paused for a beat, rocked heel to toe. "I have friends. This is my new home."

At age eight, her only awareness of home was where her body happened to be. It was not a place defined by love and security with a parent or parents, a place fixed not only in her mind but in geography. This would be the great dividing line of our siblingship.

I don't remember much more of our conversation. What kind of conversation could two kids like us have? What would we know to say to each other? I didn't know then, and neither did Malka. She spoke with a formality that felt cold and indicated pain. I tried to convey warmth, something approaching love.

And then I left.

It took Malka many years to wash away the manner and pain of our final separation. She remained at Ahava through junior high school, and then Israeli social services placed her in a foster home on a kibbutz. Despite further traumas, including sexual harassment (probably worse), this would be her most stable childhood home.

She would never return to our mother's home, and it would be another six years before I saw Malka again.

◆ ◆ ◆

My dad, Issa, Sally, Ruska, and Yosef always—and I mean, *always*—described Shraga as "a very smart man." He was soft-spoken to the point of quiet with a gentle demeanor that he used to great effect as a negotiator. Despite his disability and diminutive size, Shraga was a huge presence whenever he walked into a room. I imagine he was also a lonely man. He lived in a small efficiency apartment that shared a common bathroom; he had no wife, no children in a culture that prized family above everything else. And yet he was educated, intellectual, and connected.

When Yosef asked Shraga to help him, it wasn't a casual thing. It was asking Shraga to leverage his considerable talents and connections for my freedom and that it be among his primary concerns. He agreed and sent regular reports back to Yosef, who relayed them to Issa and my dad.

I knew little of these reports or what was happening on my behalf. I knew Issa enlisted Shraga, but Issa didn't want to raise my expectations too painfully high. My life revolved around Yosef and Ruska, school, and the Mizrachi family.

We'd met one afternoon when I took a soccer ball Issa bought me for my eleventh birthday outside and kicked it against a bare apartment building wall. I heard three girls giggling and laughing. When I turned toward them, they all started singing the lyrics of a Beatles song.

They knew instantly—as it appeared all Israelis did—that I was

American and spoke English. They came up to me, and in halting English one of them said, "Hi, I'm Tsippi, and these are my sisters, Orit and Negba."

Thus began a lifelong friendship.

In about six years, Tsippi would play a vital role in encouraging me to see Mother one last time, to ask her one last question.

While this friendship grew, Shraga's efforts began to bear fruit. Issa sent the case file from Los Angeles. As far as the State of California was concerned, Mother had kidnapped me. Then Shraga presented it to the Israeli court system in Tel Aviv. The relevant court began to see that I'd made a forced Aliyah, likely illegal, and that Mother was not fit to care for me. That she'd also lost custody of Malka helped establish her lack of fitness, too.

The next step: a court date in Israel similar to the one that had been promised in Los Angeles.

Missing from the story was Mother. There was no attempt to reclaim me, to push me to tell lies to the court, to intervene in any way. She was befuddled and wracked by illness; she had lost her daughter, she was impoverished, and she knew she was losing.

The disturbed person that I'd come to believe had no bottom or off switch had reached her end.

Because my dad was the only one with a legal claim to me, he was the only one to come from Los Angeles to Israel. When he shuffled off the plane and into the airport, he hadn't changed. His eyes betrayed the fact that he would spend the rest of his life trying to recover from the years he spent at Dachau during the Holocaust.

Dachau was the first concentration camp built by the Nazis and lasted from 1933 until its liberation by US forces in April 1945. Though not a death camp like Auschwitz, there were crematoria, regular executions, inhumane and murderous medical experiments, torture, forced labor, and starvation. The Nazis regularly sent prisoners to one of the five killing centers in Poland where the Nazis there gassed them; they pulled gold teeth, shaved their hair, and took anything else of use from the bodies before incinerating them and grinding whatever was left to dust. Despite the efficiency of these killing centers (known as extermination camps), more than 50 percent of Holocaust victims were killed in other locations, such as Dachau.

My father survived four years of this. I don't know how.

When I met him at the airport, each day he'd spent in that camp was still written in his eyes.

And yet, our reunion to bring me home to Los Angeles to live with Issa and Sally was unemotional.

I hadn't been in Israel so long that I'd forgotten he lived in a shabby studio apartment, had no wife or any money to speak of, much less a career—Issa probably had paid for his flight—and was unwilling to take any risks to improve his life. Throughout my father's life, Issa did what he could to help him but did not engage in business with him or rely on him.

By the time of his death, I was all my dad had to show for his life. "This is my boy," he'd say with outsized pride. I know he meant it as a compliment to me as much as it was to show off, but it embarrassed me because his life embarrassed me. I did not have strong feelings of love and affection for him, nor did I feel close to him. One instance in particular shows the distance of my feelings toward him. As a young man and recent high school graduate in 1977, I returned to Israel to serve in the IDF, believing it was an opportunity to grow into manhood and serve not just the State of Israel but the idea that Israel represents to all Jews. It was an outgrowth of my love for Israel that developed during my time there, especially with Yosef and Ruska. Perhaps, too, it was also from a sense of familial duty to honor the meaning of my family's suffering during the Holocaust.

My youthful ideal of heroism pushed me toward joining the paratroopers or becoming a sniper, but a hernia redirected me to the tank corps. It also led me to an IDF hospital where I had surgery to repair the hernia after about a year of service. Dad flew to Israel to be with me for the surgery. I was twenty and couldn't have cared less. I woke from the anesthesia in incredible pain, which the doctors knocked down with morphine. Dad sat by my bed each day wanting to form a connection, any kind of connection, but I ignored him, not even all that aware that I was ignoring him.

At one point, one of the Mizrachi sisters came to see me. The second she arrived, I snapped out of the morphine daze, sat up in bed, and began an animated conversation with her that lasted about an hour. Dad's pained eyes watched. He said nothing. When she left, I returned to a dour morphine haze, again ignoring him. A week later, Ruska told me, "Your father was really hurt by you. He just wanted you to acknowledge him, to be aware that he's always done his best, even if that's never been enough for you."

I was oblivious to this. This was just our relationship for most of my life. I viewed my dad as a failure, but not a loser. He was a good man; he had a lot of pride and honor, he didn't abandon me, he wanted to love me, but he had no ability to raise me. He was scared, insecure, damaged, and never took a chance in business or in life because he was so afraid of failure.

And so, I had no rapport with him.

And yet he survived Dachau. I hear the obtuseness of my feelings toward him, but this is part of the inheritance I didn't choose. He is—as with my mother—an ambiguous loss. He could never be the father I needed, desperately needed, and so I've had to mourn that as a loss and come to terms with it. How I feel about him is honest, even if it feels dispassionate or unfair.

I honor him by being true.

After the surgery, I returned to my unit in the Sinai Desert, not too far from the Suez Canal. When peace accords with Egypt were signed, the IDF reassigned my unit to a post in the Negev Desert about halfway between Egypt and Jordan. I served for a total of two and a half years that I characterize as veering from extraordinary pride to restlessness to a sense of boredom where time bled one day into the next.

◆ ◆ ◆

When Dad shuffled off the plane in 1970 to bring me home from Ruska and Josef's after my mother stole me away to Israel, he was his true self. There was no finesse about him. He was nervous and rough in the way he spoke to me, nothing like Yosef or Issa. He clearly wanted me back and was concerned about the work Shraga was doing. "Would it be enough?" he wondered.

We had a few days before the court date, and Dad wanted to do his best to be sure I was prepared. This, of course, made him anxious. "Do this . . . speak . . . come . . ." were his gruff declarations for me to do whatever he needed. I complied. All I wanted was where I believed home to be: Los Angeles with Sally and Issa.

"You need to be *very* clear with the judge that you do not want to be with your mother," he said, "and that you want to go home with your father. Don't hold back or be unsure. Be very clear. If you make mistakes, we are going to have a problem."

Yosef, though gentler, was the same way with me. "Be clear," he said often.

If he became agitated at all, Ruska was right there. "Your heart, your heart, Yosef!"

His smile would wax across his lips. "Yes, yes . . . I'm fine, yakira."

And then the day came. The judge rambled through his opening remarks, describing the case and what the hearing was to decide. Then he called me up and asked something to the effect of "You want to leave your mother's care *and* Israel?"

"Yes! I do not want to live with my mother! She lies, and she beats me! I want to go home!"

My testimony was so emotional that a reporter for one of Israel's top newspapers, *Maariv*, who was waiting for another case, wrote a feature article titled "Mother's Last Lie."

And it was. The judge ruled in my favor. For seven years I'd lived a life of fear and beatings, emotional pain, and dislocation—and just like that, it was over.

It was over, and it felt surreal. Was I relieved? Yes. Excited? Not sure. A few days later, I packed the very same child's suitcase I'd brought when Dad delivered me to Mother. Yosef joined us for the bus ride to the airport. Dad barked at me for not getting off the bus fast enough. Yosef smiled, this time with a whiff of sadness. He said more times than I could count, "We will miss you very much. You are so loved by us." Ruska said much the same numerous times as well.

Yosef walked with us to the immigration desk where our papers would be processed. The uniformed immigration officer looked at our plane tickets and court documents and then looked at Yosef. "Something's not in order," he said.

"What?" Yosef asked.

"You are missing the document that states the boy has permission to leave the country."

Yosef explained that that couldn't be right. Everything was, in fact, in order.

"No, it's not," the officer said.

I looked at the officer's uniform, his gun resting on his hip. Dad looked at the officer, then at Yosef, not comprehending what could be happening other than it was not good.

Yosef began to argue in true Israeli fashion with his hands gesticulating to make each point, voice raised. It was like a debate with a great deal of physicality, but the officer didn't budge.

Yosef, however, refused to back down.

I need to stop him, I thought, worried about his heart, worried that I'd let Ruska down. *Stop him, now!*

But I wanted to go home. Another little voice said, *No. Give him another minute . . . It's Yosef; he can do this . . .*

"The court has given approval," Yosef vented, his brow and body sweaty. "Let the boy go! You don't understand all he's been through, his father's been through . . . Let him go!"

"Enough, Yosef!" I yelled. "You need to stop. We need to go."

He looked at me; the officer looked at me. My dad stared as if he was wondering where in the world that came from. And Yosef stopped, but the damage was done.

As we walked from the officer, Yosef was sweating heavily; he seemed weakened. "I'm not feeling well," he said to Dad.

I'm so, so selfish, I thought as we waited for an ambulance to arrive and take Yosef to a hospital. *Why didn't I stop him sooner? Why am I so selfish?*

An ambulance took Yosef away. Dad called Ruska. He and I left the airport, silent.

There was one and only one sensation playing through my body, and it was GUILT.

◆ ◆ ◆

A couple days later, Dad took me to the hospital to see Yosef. His family was in his room. Their mood was soft, concerned, quiet. There were so many of them that I couldn't see Yosef at first. I expected to see tubes and monitors and ventilators and other medical devices connected to his body.

But as I pushed through, I heard Yosef's voice call out, "Let the boy in!"

I emerged into the center of this strange audience to see Yosef sitting cross-legged, with the most resplendent smile. "How are you, Mitchell?" he asked.

"Never mind me, how are you?"

He paused for a beat, then smiled at me. "Mitchell, you'll have your document soon, and sadly, you'll be leaving us once again."

"I'm not worried about that," I said. "I'm worried about you."

"Ah, Mitchell . . ."

Still, I felt deep guilt and that each person in the room knew it was my fault. I could barely look Ruska in the eye.

◆ ◆ ◆

True to Yosef's words, and Shraga's skills, we secured the document. My dad had to leave before me, but within a week of receiving the document, I was on a plane, then another, and finally landed in Los Angeles.

As much as Sally and Issa ever could or would rush toward someone, they rushed toward me. Issa hugged me, a rare thing. Sally dabbed at a tear with a tissue, and then she wrapped her arms around me and kissed my cheeks. She stood back and licked her fingertips to wipe lipstick from my face. "We love you so, so much, Mitchell," she said, her eyes tearing up.

When we walked out into the Los Angeles evening air, I felt strange. Home, but not quite at home—a sense of not being sure of belonging to a place, or if I belonged anywhere.

But I knew I was with people who loved me.

◆ ◆ ◆

Two weeks later I was watching TV in Issa and Sally's bedroom. The phone rang. Sally answered it—Issa, as usual, was at work—then screamed. "Oh no . . . oh no . . . oh no . . ." she repeated into the phone.

When Sally hung up, she walked to the bedroom and leaned her body against the doorway. "Yosef had another heart attack."

My chest constricted, prepared for her next words.

"He died, Mitchell. Yosef died." She clumsily wiped tears from her eyes, smearing her mascara.

I didn't know what to do or say. Sally left the doorway to call Issa. I turned my head back toward the TV.

Sally returned to the doorway. Her mascara was still smeared around her moist eyes. "How can you watch TV after such news?"

I had no reply for her. I was transfixed by the images on the TV and clenched the remote wondering the same thing.

Sally walked away, silent.

My one emotion: GUILT.

It's my fault. He died because of me. I'm to blame.

Sally and Issa

My father, Moshe

My mother, Giza

The only picture of my mother, father, and me that I have ever seen

Dad, Sally, and me at the apartment where I lived with Sally and Issa, across the street from the Jewish Community Association preschool

Regina—this was taken by our mother when I met my sister for the very first time, the day my dad brought me back to my mother.

Regina and me playing in front of one of the many
LA apartments where we lived with Mother

Regina and me at the last apartment before Mother flew us away
to Israel—you can see how skinny we were due to lack of food.

Sitting at the kitchen table in Aunt Ruska and Uncle Yosef's apartment—notice the affection of Yosef's arms around us both and the huge grin that he always had on his face.

Yosef and me standing by the bus that dropped us off at Ben Gurion International Airport before being denied access to leave the country—I'm holding the same suitcase that I brought the day my dad took me to my mom for the first time.

Me in my IDF uniform three months into service

Part Two

Chapter 8

NO SHIKSAS

IN HER ESSAY "Some Dreamers of the Golden Dream," Joan Didion wrote, "Unhappy marriages so resemble one another that we do not need to know too much about the course of this one."[1]

The same could be said of my marriage to Betty.

Didion acknowledges a truth that there is a plainness, a banality to unhappy marriages that makes them common, uninteresting.

To the respective spouses, of course, none of it feels common or uninteresting. A failing marriage is always a painful course of events that creates then intensify resentments, which act like cancers upon a marriage. If an autopsy were to be done, however, the results would prove the truth of Didion's statement, or at least its intention. Unhappy marriages resemble one another, so in the interest of telling a good story, let's not get into the weeds with this one.

The autopsy of my marriage to Betty—my first significant romantic relationship—would show that the lion's share of blame would be mine. It would also show that our marriage was doomed well before I first met Betty in 1980 at age twenty-one.

After leaving Mother and Israel, life with Sally and Issa was loving

---

1   Joan Didion, *Slouching Towards Bethlehem: Essays* (New York: Farrar, Straus and Giroux, 1968).

and normal. Or at least as normal as living with two scarred Holocaust survivors—and the eternal traumatic sadness of my father—could be. That said, it was impossible to expect that I could take all of the hits of my childhood and not bleed or break. Living with my broken self as a teenager and then young adult was like being a fish swimming contentedly within water: I could only notice how broken I was when I left the comfort of the water. It was then—as I transitioned to adulthood and away from Sally and Issa—that the broken me began to act out, to flail about, to harm myself and others.

Life as a kid with Sally and Issa—two doting and loving parents— wasn't always easy, but it was good. They had their wounds, I had mine, and we all kept our wounds to ourselves. My dad was the master of this.

However, as I became more and more responsible for my life and then the happiness and lives of others, the stress of it created little cracks that expanded as life applied more pressure. I acted out in my own idiosyncratic way to re-create a life of chaos that I so very much had wanted to leave behind and buried in Israel.

But these cracks were not the product of a sudden shift. They were more like evolution. People tend not to fall apart overnight. We're more like frogs placed in a pot of cool water where life turns the heat incrementally up. We don't leap out until the water reaches a boiling point, if we leap out at all.

My broken self was the water within which I lived. As I got older, life applied more and more heat.

I don't think that Betty and I ever had a chance. It wouldn't have mattered who I had met and married in the early 1980s. I couldn't take care of Mitchell Raff, so how could I live up to the responsibility of caring for a wife and child?

It didn't help that I chose to fall in love with a woman that Sally, Issa, and my father would describe as a *shiksa*.

Like so many other Jewish kids—especially the children of Holocaust survivors—I was told never to marry outside the faith. When I was about thirteen—probably younger—Issa sat me down and said, "The worst thing you could do to Sally and me is marry a shiksa."

The significance of marrying a shiksa, a derogatory term for a Gentile woman, was not lost on me.

"We suffered so much at the hands of the Nazis and all of the others who treated us so badly—many of them people we knew, friends, colleagues, parents of our classmates—all because we are Jews," he said. "I did not choose to be born a Jew, so why was I punished for that? Please, Mitchell, remember what I am telling you: Do not fall in love with or marry a shiksa. It would break our hearts."

Issa was my messiah. My goal in life was to follow his example as a person and businessman. Of course, I nodded my assent to never break his and Sally's hearts.

Through my teenage years, that proved a painfully easy promise to keep. I wasn't dating material. I was too shy, a poor student, not such a great athlete, and wasn't in with the A-list of boys and girls my age. I was a bit of a nerd and so were my friends, of which there weren't many.

Quite a few of my friends were Gentiles, which gave Sally, Issa, and my father some heartburn. I couldn't have cared less if my friends were Jewish or not.

But Sally, Issa, and my father suffered because the Gentiles they knew—the people who composed the community of their childhood, adolescence, and early adulthood—turned on them and everyone they knew. These people sent those they'd once rubbed elbows and broken bread with—fellow Poles—to their deaths out of fear, greed, starvation, and retribution. When the Shoah came for the Jews, the only people they could rely on, other than a few notable exceptions, were their own, even as they died together by the millions.

Ergo their concern that my non-Jewish friends could turn on me, even in America.

And ergo Issa's one commandment: Don't fall in love with and marry a non-Jewish woman.

It was a bias born of fear and lived experience; I got it.

I'd also experienced the many open and subtler forms of anti-Semitism practiced in the United States. In a junior high art class, I walked to a sink to rinse my brushes when a classmate whom I'd never once spoken to came up, pushed me aside, then forced my brushes out of the water. "Move over, you dirty Jew—you Jews with the big noses and kosher pickles." I was dumbfounded. *Who in the hell are you listening to at home?* I wondered. It was obvious, even at that young age, that he was influenced by adults and mimicking what he was hearing. How did he even know I was Jewish? We'd never spoken before that, and I don't believe that, with my blond hair, I looked particularly Jewish. The whole thing, to me, was a pathetic amusement more than anything else.

Another time, a manager at a popular grocery store where I was a sixteen-year-old bagger tried to pick a fight by saying, "I hate your type. You think I'm kidding? I'm not. I hate all you motherfuckers and wish they killed more of your kind. So, what are you gonna do about that?"

I said, "Whatever," then walked away wondering why anyone would make that guy manager of a well-known chain grocery store.

Then there were the casual forms of bias and anti-Semitism that will never disappear, such as mocking voice impersonations, derogatory physical representations, accusations of being cheap and greedy, misrepresentations and lies about what Zionism is and is not, accusations of disloyalty to the United States because of support for Israel, and much, much more. These are also tropes we are as likely to hear from conservatives as we are progressives, including those in and outside of government.

So yeah, I got why Issa, Sally, and my father wanted to keep the family solidly and ethnically Jewish. But I didn't agree with it. When Issa would repeat his command, I'd nod, promise, then get on with my boring, nerdish, lonely life.

I was a fish swimming in his water.

◆ ◆ ◆

In the spring of 1980, at twenty-one, I had completed my service in the IDF and returned to the United States. Like most people my age, I didn't know what to do with my life. College wasn't an option.

The biggest obstacle was me. I simply didn't have the self-confidence or self-esteem to even try. In the years before Mother kidnapped me to Israel, my school had held me back two grades while I was trying to survive her abuse and deal with undiagnosed ADHD. And then after Sally and Issa rescued me, the school district said that due to my age they would place me in seventh grade. After years of chaos with my mother, I'd only made it halfway through third grade with just a little bit of school in Israel, so I wasn't at all prepared for seventh grade. During the summer leading up to seventh grade, Sally enrolled me with a tutor to try to prepare me for school, but it was far less than I needed to catch myself up.

Therefore, no one in my life ever pulled me aside and said, "Mitchell, I think you could succeed in college." Even Sally and Issa failed to support any ambitions I may have had to go to college. They believed in me, but their support only came in the form of their love rather than encouragement to go to college. "I love you more than if you were my own son," Issa would say. Sometimes, her love for me almost overwhelmed Sally. She'd hold me tight, kiss my forehead and cheeks, then lick her fingertips to wipe away her lipstick. "I just love you so much," she'd say.

Encouraging me to pursue a higher education was never part of their love. To be fair, college wasn't part of their experience. In Poland, people stayed in their lane, and their lane wasn't one of academia. It was work and business. College was something other people—people of means and another class—could expect. When they viewed my future self, it was as a businessman in the mold of Issa.

As I considered my future after serving in the IDF, I thought I'd make a good kindergarten teacher. Then my interest in science and anatomy led me to fantasize about a career in medicine or psychiatry, which was followed by notions of becoming a psychologist. But with each of these dreams, my internal narrator spoke clearly, "You aren't good enough academically," so I didn't ever try.

Always, even to this day, I felt cheated by my childhood. Even then, I knew I was smart with a unique intellectual manner, but school never taught the way I learn. Teachers never seemed to get me, and I never seemed to get school.

I was, however, confident that I could work with my hands and was mechanically inclined. And if the Israeli military taught me anything, it was how to work hard for long hours in all conditions. Back in the United States, I toyed with carpentry, but then on a whim, I chose to go to a trade school for heating, ventilation, and air conditioning (HVAC), mostly on the cooling and refrigeration side since I lived in Los Angeles.

Issa was delighted and more than happy to pay the tuition. He also decided, "You need to get around! You can't be wasting time waiting for buses!" No test drive or haggling. Issa paid cash with a handshake for a two-door Honda Civic, and I had a car.

The final piece of the life puzzle was finding a job while I went to trade school. In an uncomfortable nod to my high school days, I was rehired by Westwood Natural Foods to run the frozen yogurt counter.

Cue the cute sisters.

In walked Celest and Betty. I noticed them right away and watched them meander around the store from the corner of one eye while I served two kids. They were pretty in a very 1980 sort of way: jean shorts, blouses, feathered hair to their shoulders.

The two kids walked off with their cones, and Celest led Betty to my counter. Like most guys my age, I was always trying to get laid but awkward at it, and I flirted with a silly, nervous energy. Celest picked up on my energy right away and responded with her own version of silly, nervous flirting.

"I'm Celest, and this is my sister Betty," Celest said.

Betty smiled and nodded to acknowledge me but said little else. She was shy, an observer who stood by and listened with amusement to Celest and me. Celest and I joked around as I gave them each samples. I learned that Celest was visiting Betty and that Betty worked at UCLA, not too far from the health food store. Once I'd served them their frozen yogurt, they paid, then turned to leave.

Celest stopped and said, "Maybe you'll see Betty again."

That was it.

A week or so later, I did. Betty came into the store, looked around a bit, then came to my counter. This time she was more at ease. She was warm and friendly, though still a bit timid.

"I remember you," I said.

"You do?"

"You came in with your sister a few days ago, right?"

"Yeah, we did."

"It's nice to see you again."

She smiled. "It's nice to see you, too." She paused. "You know, this is the only place in Westwood Village with frozen yogurt."

"Lucky me," I said. "That means you'll come back."

She seemed to appreciate that.

We talked in our awkward way for a few more minutes, then off she went. The next time she came in, we chatted for a bit about a movie we both had an interest in seeing. I asked her out, she accepted, and I thought I was going to get laid.

I took her to a restaurant called the Seafood Broiler, and as we scanned the menu, I asked, "What kind of fish do you like?"

"Oh, I'm allergic to fish."

"Um, I feel really dumb for bringing you here, I'm sorry. Do you want to go somewhere else?"

"No, it's okay. I'll find something on the menu for me."

She was still shy and wanting to please and be pleased. I liked her because she liked me.

At the movie theater we settled into our seats. She sort of leaned toward me, and I sort of leaned toward her. And then we watched *Ordinary People*: two hours of family dysfunction and suicide.

It's hard to overstate how embarrassed I was. I'd wanted romantic and mood setting, but instead ended up with traumatic and bleak.

Nonetheless, when I drove her home, Betty invited me up for tea.

Hope restored, I said, "Yeah, okay."

For two hours we sat on her couch, just two people on a date getting to know each other. I thought the longer I stayed, the more likely my chances of ending up in her bed. I enjoyed talking with her; her shyness and timidity made her easy to be with.

By about one in the morning, Betty said she had to work the next day and needed to get to bed.

"Would you like some company?"

She smiled. "No thank you, but thanks for asking and not taking it for granted like others have."

"No problem. Would you like to go out again?"

"Yeah, absolutely."

She kissed me gently when I left.

Driving home, I vowed not to initiate anything. I would wait for her to make the next move.

Four months of dating later, we were in her apartment when she said, "I'm ready."

Ready for what? I wondered. Then it hit me: SEX!

"Ready to do what?" I wanted to be coy, to force her to be a bit more explicit.

"You know."

"What? I know what?"

"You remember what you asked on our first date?"

"I do. I asked if you'd like company for the night."

"Well, I wasn't ready then, but I'm ready now."

I smiled. "After our first date, I swore to myself that I would wait as long as it took for *you* to ask *me*."

She smiled. Then this shy, wonderful young woman led me to her bedroom.

◆ ◆ ◆

If unhappy marriages are common to the point of banal, falling in love shares a certain sameness. It's the details that feel so emotionally urgent. How many unhappy marriages began because one or both partners thrived on the feeling of being loved and wanted?

I liked Betty because she liked me. I loved Betty because she loved me. I wanted Betty because I wanted someone, anyone, to scratch that interminable itch, and she volunteered. There was an emotional hole within me the size of California that I thought Betty's love could fill.

This isn't the basis of a marriage that's built to last. Yet I was willing to risk breaking Sally and Issa's hearts for a woman who was not a Jew.

Chapter 9

BETTY, SALLY, AND ISSA

HAVING A WOMAN IN MY LIFE eased my constant doubts and anxieties. Betty was like a drug, and I indulged in her as any addict would. She gave me sex, calm, and comfort. I gave her validation, companionship, and intimacy.

It felt like falling in love.

Trade school, however, soon proved to be like any other school. It wasn't for me. By the end of the second semester, the lead instructor called me into his office. When I walked in, his expression was casual as he ate an ice-cream bar on a stick. He gestured for me to sit down, so I did.

"Listen," he said, as melted ice cream dribbled down his fingers, "you failed the refrigeration semester." He licked the dribble from one finger. "I'm sorry for eating while I do this, but I have to ask you to drop out."

"Of the course?" I asked.

"No. The school."

I couldn't miss the irony of liquifying ice cream dribbling down his fingers as he told me I had failed the refrigeration class. As his ice cream melted, so did what little confidence I had in my academic skills.

It was humiliating telling Issa that I'd failed trade school, one that he'd helped me find, pay for, and even bought me a car so I could attend. He looked at me and said, "Mitchell, you're a good man. You'll figure it out."

Adding to my humiliation, I still lived with Sally and Issa and had not told them about Betty. Nor had I told Betty about my family's "no shik-sas" prohibition. Our growing relationship was more like a clandestine affair, with her apartment as the rendezvous point. She didn't mind—Betty rarely shared her opinion about anything—but I was mortified. Living a lie was one thing. Being less than a man by my own estimation was worse.

The lead instructor at the trade school had said that after some time I could reapply, but I was done with that. School was about paying to learn the theory of doing something. Experience was about being paid to learn to do something. I told Issa I would find a job as an apprentice with an air conditioning and refrigeration company.

I called every company I could find. It proved an exercise in futility. "Sorry, we're not in need of any help right now," or "We just hired a guy," or "We'd be interested if you had more experience."

After about a week of watching me feel frustrated and helpless, Issa came to me. "Mitchell, I have a friend who can help. I told him you might call."

I called Issa's friend; he laughed when he heard my circumstances, then gave me the number of a company and the name of a man. I called, and the man told me to come down for an interview the next day. He hired me on the spot as a gofer and apprentice.

I was determined to make the most of this opportunity. Not only was I quick to pick up new skills, but I learned the business side, too, and saw every mistake this guy made. I knew I could do better. After several months, and with Issa's blessing—"It's business," he said—I quit that job for another where I'd gain more experience at better pay. From there, I horse-traded my way from one company to another, picking up new skills, learning the business, and growing my confidence. Within months, I had my own apartment and was becoming more independent.

◆ ◆ ◆

If Betty was like a drug, so was work. I'd work sixty and seventy hours a week, seeing Betty in the evenings and on rare days off. It felt like growth and adulthood rather than escape, though I would learn it was both. As my therapist Ann would later say, I was drowning myself in work and Betty so that I didn't have to deal with the existential question of who I really was. There was a reason it felt good to drown.

Ann would also help make me aware that I was compartmentalizing my life. Sally, Issa, and my father were one compartment, Betty was another, and work was the third. Each its own unique entity, and within each I'd play a different role. There was the competent HVAC guy, the loving and committed boyfriend, and the loving and loyal son. It was natural for my work life to remain separate from my home life, but the longer I kept Betty from Sally and Issa, the more I was betraying them.

I knew I had to introduce Betty to Sally and Issa, but Betty never pressed. Her timid way of being meant that if she had a concern, she didn't express it. There were no questions like: "What are we doing? Where is this going? When will I meet your parents?"

At the same time, she had a strong intellectual life that included no small amount of study on faith and religion, especially Judaism. She probably knew more about Jewish culture than I did and expressed an interest in converting from Catholicism to Judaism. This was as much her walking her own spiritual path as it was a desire to be closer to me.

So, when I pulled into Sally and Issa's driveway, I was more nervous to introduce Betty to my family than I was when I had met Betty's family a month or two before. At the dinner table, her eldest brother, Jim—there were four boys and five girls—fired one pointed question at me after another. I answered what I could, deflected what I could, and eventually he backed off. The rest of the meal was normal dinner table fodder.

We stayed for dessert, hung around a little longer, then began to say our goodbyes. As we stood by the door, Betty's youngest brother, Brett, sidled up. He'd not said a word to me all evening, but he whispered in my ear, "You hurt my sister, and I will kill you."

"No problem," I replied.

"Good."

At Sally and Issa's, I told Betty to wait for a minute in the car. I hadn't yet told Sally and Issa that Betty was a Gentile.

"Where's this young woman?" Sally asked as I entered the back door into the kitchen.

My hope was that once they got to meet her, they'd love her, too. But I couldn't take that for granted, nor could I know if they'd even let her in the house. Survivorship is a tricky knot.

"She's waiting in the car," I said.

"The car?" Issa stood in the doorway to the kitchen.

I looked through the kitchen window where I could see the back of Betty's head. "I have something to tell you . . ."

It didn't go over well.

"It's not her personally, Mitchell," Issa said. "She simply is not one of us."

Sally nodded her head.

"We suffered so much back home, and suffered so much," Issa continued, "only because we are Jews. I'm sorry, this is how we feel. We cannot accept her. You need to find yourself another woman, a *Jewish* woman."

"Issa, you're not being reasonable," I argued. "How can you judge someone strictly by their faith? It's not right, and I disagree." I looked out the window and saw Betty just sitting and waiting, expecting to be let in as a guest, not rejected as a Gentile. "It's discrimination that she isn't allowed in the house. Who the hell are we to do this to her?"

I was disgusted.

Issa saw I wouldn't back down.

"Okay," he said, "I'll go outside with you and say something to her."

Issa approached the car. Betty rolled down the window and said, "Hello."

She then began to open the door, but Issa leaned forward toward the open car window. "I'm sorry, but you are not welcome in our house," he said.

Stunned, Betty settled back into the car seat.

"Here I am coming out to you instead," he added.

Issa was upset. I was seething. Betty was in shock. But that was it. Issa went back inside, and I drove Betty back to her apartment where I fell on her bed, crying. Sally and Issa were forcing me to make a choice. Would I defy them and all they've done for me or say goodbye to Betty?

I pulled myself together and looked at Betty. "I have some thinking to do." I kissed her before I left.

◆ ◆ ◆

For the next week, I kept to myself and considered what I should do next. I wondered if I was being selfish. I thought that I should honor Sally and Issa's feelings and do anything to save them from the heartache of my betrayal. *I could always find another woman*, I thought.

But at the same time, I loved Betty, and of any Gentile I could've ended up with, she was as sensitive to my Jewish identity as I could hope for. At its heart, isn't that what my family wanted? Or was it all about ethnicity, her DNA?

It was a painful process, but I concluded that given all that Betty represented and her openness to our faith, the only reason to reject her would be the accident of her birth. To reject her for being a Gentile would be wrong, so I decided I had to lead my own life, not the life of the generation that preceded me.

In so many ways, this was the most outward expression of my desire to leave behind the trauma of my parents' generation. Because of their immense suffering, they expected a certain religious and ethnic purity bordering on intolerance that I could not accept. It was yet another wound. If Betty had rejected the faith, then I—the former Israeli citizen and IDF veteran, the son of survivors, and a proud Jew—would have broken off our relationship long before. But she had not. She embraced not just who I was as an individual person but also my faith and all that being a Jew entailed.

If only it were this easy to cast off the wounds of our families.

I went to Issa to tell him my decision. "I've decided that this isn't fair." His eyes saddened. "I understand your position and need for loyalty, but at the same time, you are punishing her for something she has no control over. I get the reasoning and want to respect that, but I have my life and what I want for it."

Issa was quiet for a moment. Sally sat on the couch listening. Her eyes betrayed her pain.

"As far as I'm concerned," I continued, "you can disown me. Do what you need to. Go right ahead. If you're not even willing to give her any type of consideration as a human being, then I'm very sorry . . . for you and for me."

"No, no. You're not understanding," Issa said. "It has nothing to do with her. It has to do with *us*, with *you*."

"No, Issa," I said. "I won't fall into a belief that it's them against us and we can't mix. We are all born the same way, and we die the same way."

"Judaism is *blood*, Mitchell. It's in our blood."

I left their home believing that I'd cast aside my family, my messiah, for Betty. Looking back, I'm not sure how I expected Betty to ever live up to all that. She would be forevermore the reason I betrayed the single most important command of my family and disappointed the one man who had loved and supported me unconditionally. Even if the entirety of

Betty's and my time together had been one blessing after another, choosing her would put a lot of weight on Betty and our relationship to make up for disowning my family.

However, Issa did love me unconditionally.

Without saying a word to me, Issa met Betty at her apartment. Judaism is blood, Issa explained, and because of it, he, Sally, my father, and so many others had suffered terribly. He described what he and Sally went through during the Holocaust, and for these reasons, for her to marry me would be a betrayal—not just to my family, but to our faith.

Betty was surprised that Issa already had us engaged and at the chapel. She listened with sympathy and a well-developed sense of what it means to be Jewish. Her studies at UCLA brought her to a place where she viewed Jesus as a prophet rather than the Messiah. She explained to Issa her interest and understanding of the unique and deeply personal history of Judaism and that, separate from me and this current issue, she'd thought of converting. She described going to see a counselor at UCLA that specialized in treating Holocaust survivors and their children so she could better communicate with me and, when the time came, with Sally, Issa, and my father. She was, by her description, then later Issa's, as assertive and confident as I'd ever seen her.

Of course, like most people, she liked Issa even as he came to explain why he did not want her as part of his family.

Issa liked her, too. "That's all well and good," he said, "but our concerns aren't just for you and Mitchell. It's for the next generation, your children, as well. Will they feel Jewish? Will they feel it in their blood?"

"Yes."

Without this affirmation, I would never have married or fought so hard for Betty.

It was the survivor that rebuffed me the day I brought Betty to his and Sally's home. It was the survivor that then sent me away when I informed

Issa of my choice. But it was Issa, the man of great love, generosity, and kindness who came to visit Betty that next day.

If you were to ask me—as Issa did often, "Do you feel Jewish? Do you feel it in your blood, your heart?" My answer would always and forever be yes. I'm not religious, but I'm very proud to be Jewish. I would die for it, as I showed by joining the IDF. With this pride comes the deep need that any child of mine feel their Jewishness, that they be raised as a Jew, and that they believe they were born Jewish and will die Jewish. To paraphrase Garrison Keillor's take on Lutheranism, if they should become atheists, they would be Jewish atheists because it is the Jewish God they don't believe in.[2]

Years later, Issa often asked me about my son, Joshua. "Does he feel it? Does he feel that he's a Jew?"

"Yes, Issa. He does," was always my response.

◆ ◆ ◆

And so, Betty reassured Issa and made an almost profound impression on him. Our home and family would be a Jewish home and family.

A short while later, I made an awkward proposal of marriage, and Betty was excited to accept. We married on February 11, 1984, four years to the day after our first date. Betty was thirty, and I was twenty-five. On August 27, 1986, Joshua came into our lives. Meanwhile, I began working full-time for yet another HVAC company and moonlighting with another for thirty to forty hours each week.

I was happily drowning in family and work. The looming self-destructive crisis had not yet manifested itself in any obvious manner.

---

2   Garrison Keillor, *Home on the Prairie: Stories from Lake Wobegone* (Frederick, Maryland: HighBridge Audio, 2003).

Chapter 10

MOTHER'S FINAL ABUSE

I NEED TO WRITE OF my mother's final abuse of Malka—a final abuse of me as well—but first, I must describe what happened to Malka and our relationship after I left Israel in 1970.

Throughout junior high school—the period of my life that immediately followed my escape from Mother—I missed and thought of Malka all the time. We had different fathers, but it could not diminish my love for her, my sorrow that I'd left her behind, and the fact that she was my sister.

However, this was long before cell phones, email, and texting. The state of technology limited communication to phones or letters. Calls to Israel were expensive, of low quality, and getting Malka on the line at the Ahava orphanage was a challenge. This left letters, which, as any kid who remembers letter writing, was not a "fun" activity.

Sending each other letters was a periodic thing. I'd write, and it would take two weeks for the letter to reach Malka. A month later, often much longer, I'd receive a letter from her. Then a month later—often longer—I'd send her another letter. Our letters weren't literary or detailed correspondence. We were young and mostly described the basics of our lives. I suppose if I could go back and reread her letters, I'd also detect her hurt and anger toward me.

In one letter she enclosed a black-and-white photograph of her. "So you can at least know what I look like," she wrote. I cherished the gesture, cutting it down so it could fit in my wallet, where I could look at it many times each day. My reply included a photograph of me.

To be sure, the depth of our actual letter writing did not reflect the intensity of the emotions either of us felt. When her letters arrived, there was nothing better.

In 1976—seven years after leaving Israel and one year before I joined the IDF—when I was seventeen and Malka fourteen, I traveled back to Israel, where I stayed with Ruska. The space in her apartment and life left by the death of Yosef did not ease my broken conscience. I still felt in my heart—as I do to this day—that I was responsible for Yosef's death. I'd killed him. I didn't know what to expect when I arrived from the airport at Ruska's building and walked up the well-worn marble steps to her apartment. Instead of anger and pain, the same loving woman opened her door and her life to me. The food and family flowed as an unbroken river, letting me take no small amount of joy at being back in Haifa.

In the single-story house across the courtyard, the Mizrachi family had grown a bit older but no less happy or generous. Everyone welcomed me back into their personal world, which helped build an even greater sense of connectedness to this country, its people, and my extended family. This was the summer after my junior year of high school and played a significant role in my return a year later and the decision to join the IDF.

But for now, this was about family and—as Issa so often reminded me—ensuring that I feel, truly feel, Jewish.

Malka was no longer in Ahava. A year or so before, she had gone to live with a foster family on a kibbutz called Maoz Chaim near the Jordanian border. In usual fashion, rather than make plans to meet, I said I'd visit, and one day I found myself yet again wandering a strange compound of buildings and agricultural fields. I walked around asking if anyone knew

Malka. Someone would say yes and lead me to the next likely location. The kibbutz resembled a cross between a working farm—dairy, fields, barns, tractors, lots of kids, open grassy areas, fruit trees—and a military base—mess hall, dorms and living spaces, huge kitchen, and classrooms.

Despite being "with" a foster family, Malka lived in a dorm, and when I found her there, it was evident she wasn't happy. Her foster family had its problems, too. Years later, she would tell me that the father was a perverted, sick man who tried to molest her several times. She did not share this with me during our visit, but the tension in her body and bearing made it clear that she was in a state of hypervigilance, always wary. It also became clear that she held a lot of resentment toward me due to feeling that I had abandoned her and left her to fend for herself. During this visit, she was cold, distant, and we lacked a rapport, though she was glad that I came.

I told her that leaving her with Mother wasn't my decision. Then I explained how difficult living with Mother was for me. As the receiver of nearly all Mother's abuse, I told Malka, "You don't know Mother like I do."

For the remainder of the day, we hung out at the pool, ate at the mess hall, and she introduced me to her friends. Then I left.

◆ ◆ ◆

In 1977, I graduated from high school and—almost still in my cap and gown—boarded a plane bound for Haifa, Israel. I stayed with Ruska for a time, considered joining the IDF but was unsure if the IDF was what I wanted, then decided to try living on a kibbutz. Life was good on the kibbutz, but in Israel military service was and remains a ubiquitous aspect of the Jewish/Israeli identity. Everyone my age was in the service, and threats from the Arab nations and militant Palestinians were constant. Just four years before, Egyptian and Syrian forces had attacked Israel on Yom Kippur. In 1976, Israeli special forces freed about one hundred hostages held by Palestinian hijackers at Entebbe International Airport. The Camp David Accords were more than a year away, and the Palestinians had little intention of ending their sustained terrorist violence.

Seeing every young man and woman either about to enter the IDF, on leave from the IDF, or just ending their service, how could I not choose this course? It was not just a calling to serve the nation of Israel and all it stands for to Jews around the world, but also what my peers—people whom I respected—were doing out of duty and faith.

During this time, I traveled to Maoz Chaim to visit Malka, where we had the same cool-to-distant visit we shared the year before. She was happy to see me, proud I'd chosen to serve in the IDF, yet filled with resentment that I'd left her behind. The contrast between the lives we'd led so far was significant. There was never a guardian angel like Issa or Sally hovering nearby to help her, guide her, and express their unconditional love for her. If she had an easier time when we lived with Mother, she had a far more difficult life after Mother.

Seeing her broke my heart.

◆ ◆ ◆

In about 1979—the date is hazy, but the memory is clear—I was on leave from the IDF and visiting Ruska. As was always the case at her home, food, love, and family flowed in abundance despite Ruska's challenging financial state. And the Mizrachi family were always people of warmth, love, and generosity, despite their financial challenges as well. The fact that each of these families had enough to maintain happiness speaks to a success of Israel.

During this leave, I also made time to visit Malka. As with every visit I ever made to an orphanage or kibbutz, I wandered around for a bit asking, "Do you know Malka?" Before long, I found her, and we settled into a conversation.

"Mitch, I went to visit Mother the other day," she said.

"And?"

Her eyes wandered from mine; tears welled. "I experienced a side to her that I never knew she had. I now understand why you feel the way you've felt all these years toward her."

When she said this, I was twenty and she was seventeen, too young to navigate all we'd been through. I was happy—overjoyed, really—to hear this, but I also wondered what had taken her so long.

"I'm sorry," I said.

She looked up at me. "I'm not angry anymore. I saw it. I felt it. I want us to be closer as brother and sister."

"I'd like that, too." Our mother in her hateful, self-serving way had convinced Malka to trust me again.

We were quiet for a beat, allowing the moment—our new way between us—to settle.

"What happened?" I asked.

"I visited her to ask who my father is."

"Oh."

She described how abusive our mother became. How selfish she was in denying her daughter something so critical to her sense of self, to her humanity. It was eye-opening for Malka in an incredibly painful way. It infuriated me.

"You're the only family I have." Malka cried softly as she said this. "I love you. Let's be brother and sister again. Let's be better to each other."

"Of course. I've never wanted anything else."

Then, for the first time in our lives, we talked about what each of us had gone through with Mother. I'm not sure why it took us so long to do this. Probably geographic distance as much as emotional. Or maybe it's a way of being we'd learned from living with—beneath, sometimes—so many survivors. A stoicism that comes from the belief that nothing could be worse than the horrors of Dachau, a Soviet work camp, hiding in a frigid barn, the many other work camps, and the death camps.

Though, it became clear—especially later, when Malka would tell me of the abuse she'd suffered—that I was truly fortunate to have Sally and Issa in my life. Malka never had anyone quite like them in hers. If she had, her life would have been much less bitter and pained.

But she had me. I decided that I would do whatever I could to help her.

Reflecting on the men—many of them—that Mother was with before she became ill led nowhere. Yes, maybe one of them was Malka's father, but none of them seemed likely. And it wasn't like I could follow Issa's example when he was searching for me and hire a private investigator. I simply didn't have the resources.

The only person who knew was Mother. I had to go see her.

This was neither a quick nor easy decision to make. My service in the Israeli military limited the time I had to travel and engage in life outside of military duties and routine. I also never wanted to see her again. The last time I saw her, I stole a five-lira note and ran off to Ruska and Yosef's. There'd been no phone calls, no letters, no communication of any kind from her or me. There was no apology from her, and there would never be anything even close to rapprochement from me.

While in Israel, Ruska and sometimes Tsippi would say I should visit Mother, that she was the only mother I'd ever have. Couldn't I soften my hard heart just enough to see her, to hope that she could change? Ruska knew Mother when she was a bride candidate for my father. She'd seen something in my mother that I'd never seen, something that made her believe I should visit Mother despite all the harm she'd caused. In her selflessness, Ruska made periodic visits to Mother as acts of kindness and mercy. My answer always was polite yet firm: "No. Please don't tell me how I should feel."

"She's a sick woman, Mitchell," Ruska would say. "Go, Mitchell."

"No way, Ruska. Absolutely not. I don't miss her or care for her. I'm sorry, but I just can't bring myself to see her."

After reconciling with Malka, my position softened. There wasn't anyone else in Malka's life who cared enough to search for her father and no one with whom our mother might share that information other than me. In May 1980, the IDF discharged me from my service. I returned to Ruska's unsure of whether to remain in Israel as my home or return to Sally and Issa in Los Angeles.

I also considered whether I should visit Mother.

"Mitch, I'll go with you," Tsippi said.

"You'll go with me?"

"Yes. If that's what it will take to get you to see your mother, I will go with you."

"Okay. Then yes."

I was now twenty-one, I had served two and a half years in the Israeli military, and yet I was hesitant. If not for Malka and Tsippi, I would not have gone.

The convalescent home Mother lived in was in Hadera, a small coastal city just south of Haifa. It was much like her prior convalescent hospital—white stucco two-story buildings constructed in the 1920s with aged Spanish tiles on the roof. The buildings were made of cement for security during the British occupation of Palestine.

Inside the ward that held Mother, it felt like the stereotype of a World War II hospital: a large, open, minimalist white room with metal beds and nurses dressed in white moving about and caring for their respective patients. The floor was made of tile; there were never any carpeted or wood floors in Israel.

A nurse led us to Mother's bed, where she was lying on a thin mattress. I sat in a painted white wooden ladderback chair. Tsippi stood slightly behind me. This was a place where people go to die. There was no cure for Mother, just so-called treatment for her symptoms. There was little fresh air, and she had the skin-and-bones look of a Holocaust camp survivor. Jaundice had yellowed her skin, which was scabbed from incessant scratching, and on her head only small tufts of hair were left, some of which grew through her scabs.

It was an ugly sight, yet I held no sympathy for her. I'd come for a single purpose. I'd had enough of her. I'd had enough of not knowing. I'd had enough of what she did to me.

"I'm not here to talk with you," I said. "I'm here to find out who Malka's father is."

She frowned a little bit. "Get me back to the United States." Her voice was strong, and her mind seemed as sharp as ever even as her body rotted.

"No."

"I'll get better healthcare in the States."

"I'm not here for you to ask me for anything. Who is Malka's father?"

"I want you to speak to Sally and Issa for me. I want you to make it happen."

"Malka needs to know and should know who her father is."

"Speak to Sally and Issa; get me back to the United States. I've been writing to them. They know what I want, even if they haven't written back to me."

"I'm not here for you. I'm here for Malka. Who is her father?"

"Get me back to the States, and then we can talk about that."

"No. That's not the way this works."

She continued to talk past me, to insist that I do all I could to get her back to the United States and to have Sally and Issa pay for it all.

"You're being selfish," I said.

"No, I'm not. How could you say such an untrue thing?"

"If I leave here without the name of Malka's father, you'll never see me again."

"First, speak to Sally and Issa about getting me back to the States."

"No. For the last time, who is he?"

She turned her head away from me.

"I'm leaving." I got up and turned to walk away. Tsippi's eyes were a mix of sadness, disgust, and horror. I walked away slowly from Mother without a glance back, hoping with each step, hoping that she'd call me back, that she'd relent, that she'd say something, even a lie. *You're conniving enough*, I thought. Silence.

Mother hadn't seen me in ten years. Nothing had changed.

After we left, Tsippi never brought up my mother again. I remember her describing how she'd never experienced such coldness between two people in her life.

"I told you," I said, "there's nothing between us."

◆ ◆ ◆

A day or so later, I called Malka.

"I can't believe she'd do that," Malka said. "Thank you for trying, but why would she do that?"

Once more, she was hurt by our mother and left without any sense of resolution. Not knowing her father was like a growing tumor, the emotional effect of it metastasizing within her. She lacked an identity and father figure, which would affect her for the rest of her life. And she could not have been more different from our mother. She was kind, selfless, a giver . . . truly a good person.

She deserved so much better. She deserved to know.

After this call and my return to Los Angeles, Malka and I fell into a casual correspondence similar to what we had prior to my first visit to Israel in 1976. I don't believe it meant the bond between us had weakened. It was more the product of distance and lives led in two very different places and ways.

That changed after Joshua's birth in 1986. I wanted my sister to meet my wife and our child, for her to connect with her nephew and family. She still lived on the kibbutz and had completed two years of obligatory military service herself. Joshua was six months old when I bought her a round-trip ticket to stay for a month.

It was either the day she arrived or the next that she told me, "I don't plan on going back."

"What?" I asked.

"I don't plan on going back to Israel."

I felt duped by her; she'd interposed herself into the compartmentalized life that I'd carefully cultivated: Sally and Issa, Betty and Joshua, building a business with seventy- and eighty-hour workweeks, and a new and growing sexual addiction that included strip clubs and massage parlors. (I tell the story of this new addiction in the next chapter.) Within this life, I didn't feel there was room for another compartment.

I looked at Malka. "I bought a round-trip ticket for you to stay for a month, not a one-way ticket, and you tell me this now? How dare you do this to me! Why didn't you tell me before now?"

She looked hurt, numbed. "I thought it would be okay."

I was cold. "You can stay for a month, but then you have to find a place."

Her visit didn't get off to a good start, though things between us eased. In the end, Malka decided to go back to Israel, where she saved as much money as she could. Eight months after her first visit—early 1987—she returned to Los Angeles to make a go of it. She found a job as a nanny for free room and board, slowly established herself with one of the many Jewish and Israeli communities in Los Angeles, then became a kindergarten teacher's aide at Sinai Synagogue in west Los Angeles.

Our relationship slowly improved as she got on her feet, and I found a way to create a new compartment for her in my life. Then—hypocritically, given my growing sex addiction—I became worried about Malka's promiscuity. My theory was and remains that lacking a father and stable loving parent of any kind left a large hole in her emotional self that she tried to fill with men. But like others who've suffered through trauma, she couldn't make herself emotionally vulnerable. Committing to a single man probably felt like a step too far for her.

We'd often have the same conversations:

"I met a guy I really like," she'd say.

"Oh, that's wonderful, Malka; I'm so happy for you."

"But I'm not physically attracted to him."

Not long after, she'd break up with him, and the next time we met, she'd say, "I met a guy I really like."

"That's great," I'd reply.

"We're having really great sex, but he's the bad boy type, so he's really not that good for me."

"Oh, that's too bad."

Weeks would go by, then, "I met a really great guy, a really good guy, nice job, treats me nice."

"Let me guess, you're not attracted to him?"

She laughed. "How did you know?"

◆ ◆ ◆

At the end of January 1988, I was paying one of my usual visits to Sally and Issa when the phone rang. Sally answered. A few moments later, she called for me to come to the phone. "It's Ruska," she said.

A call from Israel was never just a call. It was still expensive and reserved only for specific times to reconnect or share important news.

"Hi, Ruska," I said. "What a surprise!"

"Mitch, I have to tell you, your mom passed away."

"When did this happen?"

"Two weeks ago."

"And you're just calling now?"

"I just found out, too. It was the hepatitis."

I felt nothing. Not happiness or relief, no sadness. Just empty. "Okay."

When I called Malka, she was shocked. We made plans to meet the next day at my home. When we were together, she said, "Mother's really dead?"

"Yes. Really dead."

She asked again, still in shock, as if she couldn't believe it. "What did Ruska say? What do you know?"

"I only know what Ruska said. Mother died of hepatitis on January 10 at the convalescent home."

"Did she say anything?"

"Mother?"

"Yes. Did Mother say anything?"

"Not that I know of."

In Malka's questions, I heard her mourning not her mother, but any chance that she'd learn who her father was. Yet another act of cruelty from our mother to Malka. Yet another ambiguous loss for Malka to navigate.

◆ ◆ ◆

Malka's way with men went on a few more years until one day in mid-1995, in a fit of frustration I said, "Your behavior toward men is nothing short of being a slut."

There was no small amount of self-hatred projected onto Malka based on my own failings and sexual addictions.

"No. No, it's not!" she said.

"Malka, look at your behavior toward men. You sleep with married men, for starters, and you yourself have told me how many men you've been sleeping with. Not only that, you're not using protection all the time either. What about AIDS? That's crazy."

She stared at me with bewilderment, as if to say, "How dare you judge me?" After a moment, she said, "You know what, Mitch? I think you're right."

A month or so later she went with a friend to a class to help Jews find themselves and learn how to get their lives to a better place and become closer to their Jewish faith.

Slowly, Malka's way with men changed. She became more interested in Judaism, little by little becoming more religious. She stopped being so quick to sleep with men, found new friends—mostly women—and became what Jews refer to as "returning to the answer," a form of being "born again." She started eating kosher and sought advice and counsel from rabbis at her synagogue. She dressed as a Hasidic Jewish woman and attended more classes and seminars that increased her connection to Judaism.

A few years later—early 2000s—she was a practicing Hasidic woman.

With her transformation, it became harder and harder to find things we held in common. By now, my sexual addiction had transitioned to include drugs (ecstasy and meth), greater sexual risk-taking (as a married man and father), a perverse and damaging affair, and, at the very least, drinking excessively. As a result, it was difficult for me to spend any time with Malka unless it had something to do with a Jewish holiday or religion.

Eventually I pleaded, "Malka, I'm asking you not to become any more religious or too crazy religious. I'm afraid it will affect our relationship."

She laughed. "Mitchell, I'm already there. I'm already what you'd call a religious fanatic."

She'd left Israel to find her birth home, but instead found her way to a more conservative form of Judaism in Los Angeles. I didn't know what to say other than, "I'll always accept and love you, no matter what."

◆ ◆ ◆

Mother's final abuse of Malka was to deny Malka the ability to marry within her faith.

As an ultra-orthodox woman, without knowing who her father was and details of his life and faith, Hasidism considered Malka a bastard child. She longed to marry, but Hasidism could not reconcile her bastard state with the sacrament of marriage.

She did try, though. She met two men—one after the other, not at once—whom she wanted to marry and who wanted to marry her. With both, she appealed to orthodox rabbis, but none of them would give their blessing or permission.

Mother's selfish refusal to share any information with Malka or me as to who Malka's father was consigned Malka to a painful choice: loneliness or leaving her faith.

Malka continued to try to choose both, but in the end, it would be loneliness.

◆ ◆ ◆

In 1995—as Malka was undergoing her transformation—I traveled to Israel for the first time since leaving the IDF to visit Mother's Israeli government-issued burial plot. The appearance—desolate and lonely—of her gravestone bothered me. In that particular cemetery, I didn't see one single government-issued gravestone other than Mother's, and there were tens of thousands of graves.

Over the next eighteen years, I'd visit Mother's gravesite several times. In May 2014—now with a measure of business and financial success—I ordered a mason to cut and install a new gravestone. It matched the many thousands throughout that cemetery.

I did not do this out of love. Nor did I do it for Mother. By then, I wanted desperately to heal, to be a better man, the man I was meant to be before Mother called out from the other side of the fence of that little preschool in 1963, "Little boy, I know your name."

From that moment on, she put me through years of abuse, abuse that set the stage for my own downward spiral as an adult.

In 1986, with the pressures of a wife and child, the stress of building an exhausting career, the complexity of loving my sister, and the expectations of Sally and Issa, suppression was no longer an effective coping strategy to deal with my fear and pain.

I started abusing myself of my own free will because I didn't know any different.

With that, I created chaos and pain.

Chapter 11

FALLING APART

THE STORY OF MY LIFE FALLING APART as an adult is presaged by something I did as a teenager.

In junior high school—I was fourteen—I came across a magazine printed on newsprint called the *L.A. Star* that published personal ads for escorts, which they advertised as "massage therapists." One evening, Sally and Issa went out for the evening, telling me that they wouldn't be back until late. I went to the garage where I had hidden the magazine and ordered a "massage" for 7:00 p.m.

At that young an age, I wasn't thinking of sex. I wasn't sure what I wanted, other than I wanted a woman to touch me. That said, I knew these ads were not quite legit, which was why I hid the magazine and my so-called appointment.

As the appointment time neared, I took my clothes off except for my underwear and wrapped my brown terrycloth bathrobe around me.

At seven, there was a knock on the front door. No one used the front door. For all I knew, it might not even open. This was enough to send me into a minor panic. I opened the door, and there was a burly man standing there, his head scanning around the neighborhood.

"Are you the driver?" I asked.

He smiled when he saw the fourteen-year-old me. "You could say that. Did you order a massage?"

"Yes."

He held out his hand. I paid him. Then he walked to his car, opened the passenger side door, and out stepped a woman in her mid-thirties, voluptuously dressed in a low-cut blouse, heels, and a black-ruffled mini-skirt. When she reached the front step and saw me—looking every bit as panic-stricken as I felt—she turned to the driver, who by now was sitting in the car. He urged her on with a flutter of one hand.

Turnover being the key to their business, she walked past me. "Where's *your* room?"

I closed the door to my room behind us. She looked around—typical teenage bedroom, posters and all—then eyed me like, *Well?* As if she expected me to be ready to get to it.

But I wasn't. Not, you know, physically. If we'd started, it would've been over in minutes, but I couldn't continue to play whatever role I had dreamed up should a woman actually appear.

"Shall we?" she asked.

"I don't know."

"You don't know? Don't know what?" She stood with a slight smile, one hip jutting toward me.

"I don't think I can."

"Sure, you can. It's nice; you'll like it."

"I think—"

"Don't think so much." She signaled with her hands, *Off with the robe, kid*, but I wasn't budging.

"I think this isn't what I want." My angst-ridden mind conjured Sally and Issa pulling up in front of the house, about to enter at any minute. "I think you should go."

She smiled. "Okay, but no refunds."

"I don't want the money. Just please leave."

I walked her out the front door and watched her stroll back to the car. She sat in the passenger seat, said a few words to the driver, and he turned toward me, laughing. She laughed, too.

When Sally and Issa came home, I couldn't look them in the eyes for days.

Many years later, my therapist Ann connected that night to my later destructive habits. She said, "Your sexual development and willingness to put yourself in scenarios are attempts to replicate the dysfunctional chaos from which you escaped as a coping mechanism. You're using it to distract—or escape—from the fear and sadness that never left. Mitchell, you were still in a lot of pain and looking for any relief you could find. It's acting out, but acting out because when we are in pain, all we want is for it to stop. When we feel like that, we're desperate and will try anything."

◆ ◆ ◆

Almost from the moment Betty told me she was pregnant in December of 1985, I lost all sexual desire for her. For the next three years, we would have sex only once.

It wasn't that I found her unattractive. Nor was it that I was unhappy in our marriage or felt some sense of buyer's remorse with her pregnancy. Intimacy—even kissing and holding hands—just went out the window.

What didn't go away was the constant sadness, depression, and fear that I'd felt since I'd lived with my mother. As I've said, these emotions were so constant that they were the water—the emotional medium— within which I swam. Only once pulled from this emotional medium could I gain the perspective to see how damaged I was, but in 1986, that was about twenty-six years away. I still had a lot of punishment to put myself and the people who loved me through.

The beginning of which occurred while driving down Beach Boulevard in Huntington Beach.

In addition to my emotional fatigue and the stress of impending
fatherhood, my seventy- and eighty-hour workweeks had taken a toll. I
was sore and exhausted beyond measure. Along this particular roadway,
there was an unusual number of massage parlors advertising in one way
or another that they held the secret to relaxation and calm.

Why not? I thought.

No, I wasn't that naive, but I needed to at least pretend that I was.
Soon after the massage started, the masseuse made it clear she was willing
to offer more.

Why not? I thought again.

As she did her work, I convinced myself that this wasn't cheating,
and then everything fell away—the stress, exhaustion, worries, sadness,
anxiety, and emotional pains melted away. For a moment, I'd left the
fetid emotional medium in which I swam.

And then it was over. Back to everything I wanted to escape.

A few days later, I wanted to experience life outside of my watery
medium again. So, I went to the same place, same woman, same deal. It
wasn't—as the jokey term goes—a *happy ending* because when done, I
was right back to where I was before. Perhaps I even felt worse for having
escaped my sadness and depression for a moment, only for the masseuse
to release me back into it.

A couple days later, I went back again. Same masseuse and situation,
same results. For the next few weeks I'd return, ask for the same masseuse, and have a similar yet not quite so successful escape. Like any good
drug, the effects faded the more I used it. To seek an escape equal to that
first session, I tried other young ladies in the same parlor. Then I tried
two at the same time.

My diminished response to the drug led from my first experimentation to dependence. I'd managed to create yet another compartment in my life that I had to hide from the people in every other compartment. And yet, despite not being happy with my behavior, I also wasn't that concerned by it.

This led to experimenting with other massage parlors, always seeking out the equivalent of that first high. I never quite found it, but I also never found the experience to not offer an escape. Like any addict, hungry for the world to melt away, I traveled from one city to the next within Orange County to try new parlors and women. Since this was Orange County of the late 1980s, there were plenty of parlors willing to offer me a respite from the reality of myself.

I was now an expert at the happy ending dance. A hand brush here, a verbal hint there, the pause waiting for me to say something, and then a deal made. Some parlors were as run-down as the stereotype of a massage parlor, while others were classy and not cheap, but even the more expensive parlors and masseuses gave off a certain vibe that communicated what was available.

Within a couple months, this was not enough of an escape.

◆ ◆ ◆

Back in 1968—I was nine and living with Mother—one of my friends lived in an apartment building with a cinderblock wall running along the back. On the other side of that wall was a parking lot that belonged to a topless bar.

One day, my friend and I snuck around to take a peek at the front of the bar. We could have simply walked around the block from his apartment building, but it was more fun and adventurous to climb over the cinderblock wall. It felt like a mission rather than a perverse curiosity. The entrance was open, with only an immodest curtain to block a deeper look inside.

I walked up to the curtain, my heart racing a mile a minute, and peeked through. The first sensation was a wonderful scent carried on the air followed by music, soft lighting, and a beautiful topless dancer about twenty-five feet away looking straight at me. A wan smile spread across her lips, and I ran away for all I was worth.

Despite that impulse of fear at the dancer catching me with her eyes, I was amused, excited, and intrigued by what I experienced. Another day, I went back, and as I approached the curtain, I was equally as intoxicated by the scent, music, and risk as before. I moved the curtain aside, but then a man grabbed me from behind, lifted me into the air with the greatest of ease, and gently placed me on the sidewalk away from the entrance. Without a word, he turned and walked back to the bar's entrance.

I ran away, and though I never returned, I remained curious.

As with the massage parlor, I was driving down Harbor Boulevard in Santa Ana when I noticed a sign for one of these clubs. And as in the past, I thought, *Why not?* with the same willful and false naivety. Another thing that had not changed was my fear and anxiety of being "caught" in such a place. By "caught," what I really meant was being seen by anyone. I walked in quietly, almost like a burglar creeping into a house, then sat in the back to attract as little attention as possible, especially from the dancer. As in 1968, the thought of her eyes catching mine remained.

I drank a beer, watched for about twenty minutes, then left.

The seed had been planted, and the next aspect of my sexual addiction was born. A day or two later, I returned to the same bar, this time sitting a bit closer, staying a bit longer. Days later, I visited the same bar, but I sat closer, drank two beers, stayed longer. And so, it progressed until I sat at the front of the stage so I could drop money on the stage floor and the women would come to me like bees to honey. I soon collected a set of favorite dancers at several other strip clubs. They learned not just to recognize me but what moves would get me to tip more and more. It became a tease and seduction I was more than willing to participate in.

With the development and growth of this new facet of my addiction, I was still visiting the massage parlors. Eventually I wove the two together, with one feeding the other to intensify the sensation of escape. To mitigate my growing tolerance for this drug of choice, I visited more and more clubs and parlors until I knew nearly every single one of them within Orange County. No matter how small or out of the way an establishment was, I'd find it.

Of course, with all the time I spent in strip clubs, the amount I drank increased. I never drank at work, only moderately around Betty and Joshua, and rarely around Issa and Sally.

Within a year I was out of control. One masseuse told me I was insatiable because there were times when I wouldn't allow the masseuse to bring me to climax. I did everything I could to stay at the peak, the just-before place when I was in a state of total escape. I would go to a strip club where the women would tease me as I drank a beer or two. Then I'd go to a parlor where I wouldn't let them push me over the edge into climax. Sometimes, I'd ask another masseuse to step in and start another hour-long massage to tease and torment me, but I wouldn't allow them to finish me. Then I'd go to another strip club and repeat the process all over again.

There were times when a masseuse would ask why I didn't have a girlfriend with whom I could do this.

"I don't know," I'd say. "I'm married, but . . . I don't know."

"That's okay," the masseuses often said. "You're a nice guy and a good tipper."

I was a willing and eager masochist, willing to do whatever it took to prolong my escape, to live outside the emotional medium that was my normal state.

To say the least, it was a maladaptive coping strategy. It was a trick I was pulling on myself to escape my past pains and current stresses. It was avoidance, too—avoidance of doing the work of healing that I needed to do.

At the same time, it was only one of my compartments. Just as I fully engaged with this compartment when I was in it, I was fully engaged when in the other compartments of my life. I was attentive to Betty even without making love. I was as much of a father to Joshua as any father when I wasn't working, visiting bars and parlors, or spending time with Issa.

Obviously, a "good" husband does not do these things. A "good" father does not live this life. A "good" professional and entrepreneur does not distract himself from his work in this way. A "good" son does not engage in this level of deceit.

But I did my best. The result being no one in any of the other compartments was aware of my addiction or my internal need for escape. And the more I escaped, the more I needed to escape because every pain— past, present, and future—only got worse the more I ignored them.

My state of denial was profound.

◆ ◆ ◆

In late 1987, I sought out my first therapist, Mariana.

The logical and expected reason would be that living in denial of my sexual addiction could carry me only so far. It had seeped into my conscious life in a way that I could not ignore, that would trigger the need for help.

But that's not why I started therapy. Since about age five, my affection-starved brain daydreamed of idealized expressions of a mother's love. Especially thoughts of a romanticized mother figure holding and cuddling me. One could draw a very short and straight line between my sexual addiction and these daydreams, but this fixation was utterly asexual. It could and should be read as the expression of a deep, unmet need for sensory regulation and unconditional love.

Whatever it was and however anyone would perceive it, it was a fixation, and that meant for the entirety of my life, it was insistent and unyielding to the point of being exhausting.

In my first few sessions with Mariana, I described this unmet need as the reason I sought her out, then explained a bit about my past and my current life, which included visiting strip clubs and massage parlors. Being a good therapist, Mariana immediately identified my sexual addiction as an unhealthy coping mechanism connected to my childhood and started treating me for it. Much like in a twelve-step program, she'd start each weekly session by asking if I had engaged in my addictive behaviors the prior week. Then we'd spend much of our time exploring my childhood.

One day in early 1988—a few months after I started seeing her—Mariana asked, "How's your marriage?"

"Oh, shit. I think my marriage is in trouble."

This is why I say that the state of denial I lived in was so profound. Until that moment, I hadn't connected my addictive sexual behaviors to my marriage. I'd managed to so effectively compartmentalize both that I quite literally saw them as two separate and unrelated things.

I have no answer for why. It's just the truth. To paraphrase Mariana's reaction, "Hey, dummy, what took you so long to figure that out?"

Betty and I had never opened a joint bank account. We never had any conflict or drama like most couples. We never let friction or confrontation last more than a few moments. And we fooled ourselves into thinking this was good. We even bragged to other couples how well we got along and how happy we were.

The truth was that Betty had accepted me, but she never trusted me with her deepest self. I accepted her but never trusted her with my deepest self. Neither of us ever allowed ourselves to be vulnerable with each other. And Betty's passivity in the face of my control issues—we went where I wanted to go, watched what I wanted to watch, ate what I wanted to eat, etc.—seemed a complementary personality trait rather than an imbalance.

Further, what evidence did *we*—underscore the word *we* because Betty had no idea what I was up to—have to think there was a problem? We lived in a nice home in a nice community, loved and doted on Joshua, never argued or fought over money (or anything else), and so on. By all appearances, we *were* happy.

The problem was, I had never fallen in love with her. I'm not sure she had fallen in love with me, either. But we both were in love with the image of ourselves we'd created. It was an image of happy home, family, wife, career . . . but when you're broken, that formula doesn't work. What we'd instead found in each other was our opposite with complementary, not matching, personal and emotional baggage: She was a doormat, and I was a control freak.

Over the course of that session with Mariana and then subsequent sessions, I realized two things: 1) it wouldn't have mattered who I married because I was too broken to be married to anyone, and 2) we needed to get a divorce.

That said, I would never, ever back out of being a father. I loved being a father and, in particular, I loved being Joshua's father. Every single day when I came home for work, I went straight to Joshua and began playing with him no matter how hungry, dirty, and tired I was. When he entered his toddler years, I'd clean up enough to slip under the covers with him to read until he fell asleep. Sometimes I fell asleep before he did. Like Issa and Sally, my constant refrain was, "I love you so much I could eat you alive!" One day, when Joshua was about four, he started to cry and had a panicked look in his eyes. "Please, Daddy, don't eat me!"

And of course, one of the hardest days was the day I moved out of our home for good. I held him for as long as I could, telling him, "I'm so sorry, so sorry, so sorry . . ." I put him down, and he began to sob in that oh-so-painful way of a toddler, so I picked him up again and held him close. I carried him to his room and placed him on his bed. My heart was breaking. When I turned to walk away, it killed me that he couldn't understand why his family was breaking apart. But there was nothing I could do or say that would mend his breaking heart. I thought, *I wish I had the magical power to instantly show him the days and weeks and years that are to come to prove, "Look, I'm still here, I still love you so very much, I'm still raising you, I'm still part of your life."* But during those seconds, I walked away with his wailing, wet sobs behind me.

Once outside the house, I cried harder than I ever had. There was nothing I wouldn't do for my son. I would kill or die to protect him and his happiness. However, remaining married to his mother was the one thing I simply could not do.

From the moment Mariana first asked, "How's your marriage?" to the day I asked for a divorce took three years. I was just too afraid to ask. After what I'd been through and despite knowing that Betty was an infinitely better mother than my own mother was, I knew the implications of divorce on a child.

◆ ◆ ◆

In April 1987—the same year Malka moved from Israel to Los Angeles and I started seeing my therapist, Mariana—Betty and I moved into a newer and nicer home in Van Nuys, near Los Angeles. Instantly, my connection to the massage parlors was broken, and with that, my need for them ebbed. Where there had once been massage parlors in the same abundance as corner mini-marts, now there were just mini-marts.

Thinking back on it now, it's amazing that such an intense addiction could be broken by such a simple thing: a change of context.

However, that didn't break my need for escape. When one expression of an addiction evaporates, the remaining expression will expand to fill the void.

Visiting the strip clubs became more intense. It wasn't just a matter of a couple beers a couple times a week. With our move, my career also improved to the point that I had my own HVAC business. I was its first and only employee. Because this line of work is dependent on Mother Nature, there were times the workflow ebbed, and when business was slow, my depression and need for escape increased. For days on end, I'd sit in the club, drinking one beer after another and tipping the women and barmaids more and more extravagantly as each learned my ways and gained more seductive power. When business was good, the busyness of it offered some distraction, but I still made time for the clubs.

And yet, the void within my soul I was trying to fill demanded a greater distraction, a more powerful escape.

A new expression of my addiction would emerge before too long, and her name was Lee.

Chapter 12

LEE

NOT TO LEAN TOO HEAVILY on Joan Didion, but if stories of unhappy marriages share a similar banality, so do stories of infidelity.

And yet, the pain was intense and real for Betty and Joshua. It was anything but common or cliché. Their lives were torn apart by my deceit—a deceit that left real wounds.

Lee was nineteen when I met her a few months after the move to Van Nuys in mid-1987. Joshua would celebrate his one-year birthday that August, I was twenty-eight, and Betty would turn thirty-two . . . We were a young family.

For whatever reason, when Lee and I met,[3] she developed an interest in me and I in her. In some ways it was similar to how my interest in Betty developed: She liked me, so I liked her. When we saw each other, we'd talk. These conversations lasted a little longer and became a bit more intimate—not sexual, just close. The regular tone of her voice was quiet and fidgety but also flirtatious. She guessed from the dismissive tone in my voice that I was unhappy in my marriage.

---

3   I am intentionally vague on how Lee (not her real name) and I met to protect her as well as anyone else I could harm by telling my story.

Our meetings were intermittent, unplanned though expected because our paths crossed with some regularity. About a year after our initial meeting—in mid-1988, soon after realizing that I no longer wanted to be married—her playful way of speaking to me and the look in her eyes inspired me to invite her for a jog. This was something I would do once or twice each week along the beach near the Santa Monica Pier. It was my only healthy coping tool. The irony that I was about to tarnish it was not lost on me.

Lee said yes.

I rationalized my growing closeness to Lee by convincing myself that my marriage was pretty much over. Of course, Betty had no idea we were doomed to divorce because I hadn't yet told her. Lee was in her compartment while Betty and our marriage existed in another, separate compartment. My therapist was the only compartment of my life that had an inkling my marriage was over—that is, *pretty much* over. Even though I came to this realization with Mariana in early 1988, it took me three years to tell Betty.

The first run along the beach went well. Our verbal intimacy grew, but there still wasn't a physical intimacy between us. She was sweet and had a crush on me, which fueled me. I'd found a mechanism of escapism that intoxicated me and worked as well as my first forays into massage parlors. Under its influence, I was unwilling to consider the ramifications of my actions. I had no thought of letting Lee go or doing the right thing. At that point in my life, anything that held back sadness, anxiety, and depression was *the right thing*.

Our beach runs became a weekly routine. After one of our runs, with the sun setting over the Pacific, I asked, "Where do you see this leading?"

Despite her youth, she seemed to be the one in control, the one dictating the pace, the manner of what I assumed was a mutual seduction.

The excitement of it felt similar to the seduction within the massage parlors, though without a financial transaction.

She avoided my question, but afterward our conversations became more sexual in tone and intention.

I can't recall how many months it took before we arranged to have sex, though she'd turned twenty-one when it happened. Lee had told me she was a virgin, which I couldn't be sure was true, but she did seem immature and inexperienced. She said her lone sexual encounter did not end with him entering her "all the way." I wasn't sure what she meant by that; she was a little vague. No matter. She said she was willing to lose her virginity to me, and I was a willing participant.

I told Betty the usual lies of a cheater, something along the lines of "off to work for the day, won't be home until late." Lee and I met, spent the day together as if on a date, then made our way to the modest hotel I'd selected. In the room, I expected her to be nervous, a little scared, and I asked if she wanted to cancel the whole thing.

"No way. I'm good," she said.

Despite the confidence in her words and voice, she seemed a bit distant; she never showed me much affection or desire, which troubled me. *Maybe it's just nerves*, I thought. *Maybe she's not sure how to act.* We started kissing, got into bed, had sex, then remained with each other for another hour or two. During all of it, she lacked passion, warmth, and any sign that she was excited or turned on. We got along fine, and she was engaged in what we were doing, but the only real moment of enthusiasm from her was when she said she couldn't wait to tell her friend she was no longer a virgin.

Despite my disappointment in her lack of warmth, our rendezvous became part of my sexual addiction that still included the strip clubs. Despite the disappointing nature of our first sexual encounter, Lee soon discovered her sense of adventure and enthusiasm for our trysts. We'd plan to spend hours at a hotel room, often becoming more experimental and bolder in our sex. I found her to be a partner in crime, a fellow addict, and trusted her with my life in the strip clubs. At first, she didn't seem to care. Sometimes she'd ask about them, but during one of our hotel hookups, she asked, "Why do you still go to them? Let me do what those girls do for you."

When she said that, she opened a new door. Yes, she could do for me what those other women did. We called this "playing bar," which expanded to other sexual role-playing, which included her also coming with me to the clubs. And so, these two compartments of my life, and addiction, became one. While I'd found a new, even more powerful escape drug, when I wasn't using, I was in misery. Betty never suspected a thing, but the guilt I felt was intense. The shame caused me to drink more than I usually would. Lee would drink a little but for the most part remained sober.

After a few months, Lee and I started to quarrel. After a year, we started to fight. But neither of us could stop. Neither of us wanted to stop. The need for escape was intense. It was far greater than the guilt.

Throughout our marriage, Betty and I never raised our voices to each other. The only time I did raise my voice was when Betty's father took financial advantage of her, and I was angry with him. On the surface, all looked placid, no problems, a young and happy family.

Obviously, there were deep and terrible issues, all of them my fault. All of them creating a daily sensation of chaos that I despised but could not find my way to end. Mariana and I met off and on, and I was incredibly honest about what I was doing. She was clear that I was acting out, causing harm to my family—even if Betty and Joshua were unaware—and to my emotional and moral well-being. For three years I'd known I needed to divorce Betty, for her own sake if not for mine, but I was too cowardly to act on it. I'd complain to Mariana while also trying to dismiss, intellectualize, and fret about the hurt asking Betty for a divorce would cause.

Finally, Mariana said, "Let's bring Betty in," and I agreed.

In August of 1991, Betty accompanied me to a session with Mariana. Betty seemed nervous but also perhaps a bit relieved to meet Mariana and become involved with my therapy. For the past three years she'd not asked about my sessions other than to say, "How's therapy going?"

"Great! Really helping!" I'd reply, then change the subject.

She never seemed to mind my avoidance of the topic. It also never seemed to bother her that we'd not had sex since she became pregnant with Joshua. He would celebrate his fifth birthday on August 27.

Mariana began by introducing herself to Betty and then gently brought up that I was unhappy in our marriage.

"Unhappy?" Betty asked.

Mariana looked at me. Betty looked at me. I looked at Mariana.

"Mitchell?" Mariana asked.

I just stared at Mariana, frozen in my own cowardice.

"What Mitchell has been talking about is that he believes your marriage isn't working," Mariana said to break my silence.

"What?" Betty asked.

Mariana looked at me. Betty looked from Mariana to me, then back to Mariana, unsure who was going to speak next.

My eyes wandered from Mariana. "I can't be married to you any longer."

Betty froze for a moment. Her lip quivered; her eyes watered. It took her a moment to understand what this session was truly for. I didn't ask her to come because I wanted Betty to participate in my therapy. I asked her to come because I wasn't man enough to ask for a divorce and needed Mariana to do it for me.

When it all became clear, tears ran down Betty's cheeks. She said, "I've got to get out of here." Then she stood up and walked to the door.

Mariana turned. "Betty—"

The door shut. Betty had left. Her world of make-believe and denial came crashing down, and it was too much for her. She had been there all of ten minutes. In the wake of her leaving, Mariana paused in silence before telling me I had to go home and speak with Betty. She encouraged me to be honest, to let Betty know everything, to honor her with the truth of who I'd been and still was, that I was too wounded to be the husband she imagined me to be and that she needed.

When I got home, Betty was there. Tears still ran down her cheeks. "For three years, I thought you were working on yourself, but you were working on divorcing me."

"Yes."

I was the bad person. I was a coward. I was a liar. I was a cheater. I was as far away from being the man I wanted to be as I had ever been. But at the same time, Betty had convinced herself that a sexless, emotionally empty marriage was okay, something she could live with and even cherish.

I didn't say a word about the massage parlors—the one act of addiction I'd managed to break—the strip clubs, or Lee. Lee would simply appear one day as my new girlfriend, but by that point Betty had woken up. Lee added fresh pain to Betty's already difficult time with our divorce.

Not long after the session, Betty and I agreed to a trial separation of a month. I knew it was a lie. I wasn't ever going back. I'm sure Betty knew it was a lie, too, but she acted as if we'd only be apart while I worked through my issues.

Soon after, I asked for a divorce.

One thing I would not give up was being a father. Betty had discussed moving to Orange County to be closer to her family, which would have had the effect of separating me from Joshua. I told Betty that I would not be a weekend father like my own father was. "If you think I'm only going to be an every-other-weekend dad, no way. I'm either all in or all out."

"What does that mean?" Betty asked.

"We share custody and co-parent, or I can't be in his life."

She agreed and decided not to move. I think she felt some relief that she'd keep me as a parenting partner, and in our conversations about Joshua, we agreed to be the best parents toward him that we could. For what it's worth, as painful as the breakup of Joshua's family and the emergence of Lee into his life, Betty and I became solid divorced co-parents.

Before I moved out, Betty and I agreed that I'd find a small apartment nearby and Joshua would alternate nights between our homes. Soon after I moved out, we realized that arrangement was too tough on Joshua, so we kept him on two-night shifts. Even still, Betty and I both saw him every day, and Joshua never became a control battle between us. Our lives revolved around him. Despite my addictions and the more insane behavior to come, Joshua was always first and foremost. I kept my silent promise to Joshua on the day I left our family's home for the final time: *In the days, weeks, and years that are to come, I promise you that I am still your father; I am still here; I still love you so very much; I'm still an important part of your life.*

In May of 1992, Betty and I finalized our divorce.

As time wore on, Betty dusted herself off, made the best of her life, and settled into an amicable divorce from me. And that became my next compartment: Amicably Divorced Mitchell. There was a lot of chaos to come, but I kept all that in the Mitchell Master of Personal Chaos compartment. I don't know how I managed it, but the amicably divorced father compartment never met or ran headlong into the dysfunctional sex addict compartment.

All Betty and Joshua would ever see was Mitchell the Well-Dressed Poser.

◆ ◆ ◆

Once separated and divorced, I was free to go to the strip clubs on nights I didn't have Joshua. My desire for these women to tease me with their bodies was insatiable. Some nights I would drive from club to club until I found at least one dancer to watch, drool, and humiliate myself over until closing time. Sometimes I was so intoxicated that I didn't dare drive home. I'd lie in the front seat of my car, pass out for a few hours, then drive home before sunrise. When I'd wake up to go to work, my body still reeked of alcohol.

When work was slow—usually during Los Angeles' mild winters—I'd get to my favorite bar when they opened at eleven in the morning. I'd sit there until late afternoon, only a mile from my home.

For me, my enemy was free time. If I could not stay active, busy, distracted, or escape into my addiction, depression was on my doorstep to fill the void. I think this is why I could remain engaged in Joshua's life, start and successfully run my own HVAC business, maintain a dysfunctional relationship with Lee, and be present and adoring for Issa and Sally. I was frantically trying to escape my own head, and within this mix of healthy coping skills were the self-destructive yet incredibly effective methods I'd developed.

More on why Lee was so unhealthy in a moment, but even as I was living this life to a marginal degree of success, I knew I was in rough shape emotionally, physically, morally, and spiritually. Soon after the divorce, I reached out for help. A doctor prescribed an antidepressant—perhaps Mariana led me to this form of treatment—and for the first time in my life, I was able to not feel sad or depressed.

However, peace and calm came at the price of side effects. These included headaches and impacted my libido and ability to climax, leading to erectile dysfunction.

For a sex addict, the latter three were simply untenable. I chose to go off the meds and fight my depression and sadness through sheer force of will. I have had to fight both every day since. Though, as I write, my success rate has climbed steeply to the point that most of the time I can keep both at bay. Nonetheless, they are always on my doorstep.

My next therapist, Ann—the woman I credit with helping me finally heal—called me a well-dressed poser, but she also called me a runner. "You can go anywhere on the planet, but you're never going to outrun your problems," she said often. "Wherever you go, there you are with everything you started running with. More often than not, that baggage gets heavier and harder to carry. Never easier."

With the end of the medications, I started reading self-help books. I knew I was a mess and needed to heal. The self-help industry offered a promising do-it-yourself set of methods and practices to do that healing. Yes, I kept up with therapy, but my focus shifted to self-help practices that grew to include seminars, journaling, retreats, and whatever else I could find that I thought might help. Living in Los Angeles, there was no shortage of self-help therapies and modalities to choose from.

In the end, despite the promises of the books and the promises I made to myself, I would be the healthiest wellness guy I knew during the day but then at night go off to strip clubs or spend time with Lee. As time passed, I needed to be drunk to be with her to drown my shame, self-hate, and the fact that, frankly, she was an incredibly difficult person to be with. And then Lee introduced meth, cocaine, and ecstasy into the mix. On my own, I'd never have experimented with these drugs, and I never used them unless I was with Lee, but the drugs were like rocket fuel for our brand of crazy.

Lee was just as damaged as I was. Her childhood was tough with a domineering father that expected too much from her and withheld his love if she couldn't meet his expectations. He was also crass, vulgar, and rude. When Lee was about ten years old, he lost all interest in her. Meanwhile, her mother hovered over her like the best of all helicopter parents, to the point where she still cut Lee's food for her at age fifteen. Her mother quite literally did everything for Lee, which meant Lee never learned to be independent, think for herself, or have any self-confidence. Her mother was always right there to take care of everything for her.

Lee's father loathed the person that Lee became and blamed her mother's overweening ways for it. Her mother resented her father's behavior and emotional abandonment of the family. Together, they each held a toxic mix of resentments that left Lee with an overbearing mother and a distant father from whom she never received any love.

This poisonous environment—which lasted well into her forties—left Lee in a state of arrested development, an incorrigible and emotionally stunted young woman.

Like me, she was a wounded and broken person trying to navigate life with a maladapted set of tools.

◆ ◆ ◆

Through the late 1980s and 1990s, my business grew, and I managed to achieve a certain degree of financial security. An important piece of that was frequent and generous infusions of cash from Issa. It wasn't unusual for him to help Betty and me with the purchase of a home or money for expenses. After our divorce, when I'd visit, he always handed me what he called a "shot in the arm." This could be a few thousand dollars. With his support, connections, and business guidance, I became a very busy HVAC contractor.

That's why when Lee said she wanted plastic surgery for her breasts, I said I'd pay for it with the exception of one thousand dollars. I wanted her mother and father to kick in that money to show that they were on board. If something went wrong with the surgery, I didn't want her parents blaming me.

They complied. Of course, Lee and I received surgical referrals from our favorite strippers. By this point, I was fed up with Lee. I told her that as soon as she had her new boobs, we were done.

We were in a constant cycle of fighting, breaking up, then going back to each other because neither of us could live without the chaos we mutually created. I would look for things to get upset over and then use them as excuses to self-sabotage not just our relationship, but also our breakups. Every fight was a breakup. There was no quarreling as couples do. It was full-on screaming at each other followed by another breakup that would last for an hour, a day, a week, a month . . . but rarely more than a couple months.

I never got what I needed from Lee other than emotionless sex, drugs, alcohol, and satisfying my deranged craving for constant insanity. She never got what she craved either except for her deranged need for constant insanity. We'd often meet at hotels—even when we didn't have to—and the instant we entered the room, I was angry at myself for doing this again. I'd mix a drink, then drop some meth into it to get high. She'd snort cocaine, sometimes meth, and we'd use ecstasy at times as well.

But rather than ease my anger or at least stop my self-loathing, the alcohol and meth ramped up both, and an insistent need to create a scene would win out. Our screams and insane behavior brought the police a few times. One time, I called 911 because in the heat of our fighting Lee threatened to kill herself and refused to leave my house.

I was a mean drunk. No violence, but plenty of verbal and emotional abuse. The next morning I'd know we'd had another of our classic fights but not remember the specifics. Because Lee hardly drank, she'd tell me the abusive things I said to her.

"No way," I'd reply.

"Yes, you did. You were really nasty to me, and rude."

I would hate myself for being such a lowlife, for acting like such a vulgar and cruel drunk. This was not the person I wanted to be. This was not the person that Issa and Sally loved so much.

Our behavior humiliated me. We were the messed-up, screaming, crazy couple. It was pathetic. She brought out the worst in me; I brought out the worst in her. We brought out the worst of each other's childhood wounds. We tapped into the other's fear, rage, jealousy, self-loathing—all the petty, bad stuff we carried.

Pushing Lee away was like an aphrodisiac to her. Whatever validation, thrill, or itch she needed me to scratch intensified during our breakups. During one fight—unbelievably we had moved in together for a brief period—I threw all of her stuff out on the front yard and driveway in front of our neighbors. Then I locked the doors with her outside sobbing, pounding on them, and yelling, "Let me back in, you bastard! Let me back in!"

Eventually she picked up most of her stuff and left for her parents' dysfunctional home. A few days later, she found an unlocked window and climbed into the house with a puppy in hand. I took her back.

We each played a particular role in our fights. I was the self-hating meth/alcohol rage-aholic. She was the self-loathing baiter and negative attention-seeker. We were in a perpetual negative feedback loop that always reached a crescendo when I would walk out screaming, "We're through. This time I mean it!"

After each breakup, her lack of self-worth would kick in hard, and she'd need to figure out a way to get me to love her again.

I'd calm down after a few hours, days, weeks, months . . . but then the loneliness, sadness, and depression would come back. She was persistent with phone calls, notes, emails, and so on, and I'd succumb to it. She never once broke up with me. This was our routine every . . . single . . . time.

This game went on for more than two decades.

In the midst of our breakups and makeups—in 1997 I met a woman named Florence. When we met, she was separating from her husband. She was the third-highest executive of a $200 million building hardware company and a well-respected and shrewd businesswoman. One article in a business magazine described her demeanor and negotiating skills, saying she was an ice queen who ate nails for breakfast.

In truth, she hated this portrayal. She volunteered for the Red Cross, loved her daughter immensely, and had a much softer side that she believed she could never expose lest it make her vulnerable in a man's world.

I respected the hell out of her. Nothing sexual, just pure respect for her as a person and business professional.

Lee hated Florence immediately. Florence's confidence, success, poise, and skills threatened Lee to no end.

Not long after becoming friends with Florence, she and I hatched a business plan devoted to providing specialized tools for the building trades. She left her company, and I left behind my HVAC business. The work was intense, with long hours, a huge amount of risk, and lots of travel. After about six months of this—with Lee and I battling the whole way—I realized I hadn't visited a strip club since I started working with Florence. Thank God.

All my money went into the business. If not for Issa's financial support, I would've lost my home and not had the financial resources to keep working on the project.

At first, it seemed our business concept would work, but then it began a slow fade. As we lost one bid after another and our sales could not make up for expenses, we sunk more of ourselves into the effort. Issa was always there to support me. He even came up with eleven thousand dollars to help me settle a lawsuit.

Throughout, the tension between Lee and Florence continued to build until Florence baited Lee into a huge fight. Lee blew her top and tried to run Florence over with her car, even chasing her down the street. Florence pressed charges, and Lee had to go to court with her father to defend herself.

Florence and I started arguing. I broke up with Lee, and then, as always, took her back. Many mornings I arrived at work hungover from another of Lee's and my sexual routines. The business failed in 1999. The dream evaporated. Florence went her way, and I went mine with Issa ensuring I had the financial resources to slowly rebuild my HVAC business.

Afterward, I vowed no more strip clubs, and I kept that vow. I also promised myself not to rely on Issa again and make my own way financially, a promise I mostly kept. I also pledged to end things with Lee for good. I did—or so I thought.

Then in late 1999, out of loneliness, stupidity, desperation, and a whole lot more pathetic excuses, I decided to reconnect with Lee. I'd felt shame and humiliation and a powerful desire to be finished with her, but I was addicted to our insanity. It was like a god to me that filled a spiritual and emotional need. It was one hundred times the escape and distraction that massage parlors and strip clubs ever were.

During the first few months, we got along well. I began to think of all the years Lee and I had been together and how much we'd been through—the good, the bad, the really bad. I also began to think that I should put my best foot forward and really commit to Lee by giving marriage a try. Lee agreed, saying, "Yes, let's focus on each other."

I came up with a plan that we'd move in together and I would give Lee the diamond ring Sally gave to me—I found out years later the diamond was glass. We would see if we could work out our issues. We would give ourselves a year of living together before marrying, which I described to Lee as the two of us flying on an airplane together that would not land for one year. "We won't be able to leave each other for the entire year," I told her. "For better or worse, we'll need to work our problems out together. If we make it through that year, we'll marry. If not, we'll call the whole thing off."

We moved into an apartment together, and for the first four or five months, things worked, more or less. However, one issue that had bothered me for the entirety of our off-and-on relationship was Lee's lack of affection toward me. She could be cold and distant, which also affected our lovemaking. Sex with her came to feel more like a service she provided than an act of love and passion. For me, this was a deal breaker that needed to change.

When I brought this issue up, we argued, it got nasty, and I ended up telling her I'd give her a month to figure out what the problem was, or I would call the engagement off.

The month went by without Lee making any effort to resolve or address what was bothering me. True to my word, I told her, "I'm done. I can't marry you."

She flew into hysterics, and soon we were engaged in one of our biggest fights. She and I were a perfect match when it came to knowing how to reach each other's deep, dark, painful places. In the midst of the fight, Lee called her mother. Soon, her mother and father were in our apartment trying to talk me out of ending the engagement.

It was a cheap melodrama from start to finish. Lee's mother and I sat across from each other at the dining room table. Lee and her father stood behind her mother. Her mother and I attempted a calm, civilized conversation while Lee's father physically restrained Lee to keep her from hurling herself into the middle of the conversation. Lee's mother and I did our best to ignore Lee.

That her mother, with Lee in a rage and physically restrained behind her, could calmly try to convince me to marry her daughter amazed me. The state of denial was frightening. I was clear, however. "There's no way I am going to marry your daughter. We're done."

After about half an hour, Lee's mother accepted what I'd said. Her husband escorted Lee out of the house to their car, returned inside to help Lee's mother pack some of her belongings, and then they left. I believed that I would never see Lee again.

A few months later Lee called, and just like that, our little clown car of dysfunction continued to wobble down the road.

◆ ◆ ◆

All the pathetic madness between Lee and me did not occur in a vacuum. Life continued around us. As I worked to escape depression and sadness, life kept piling on more depression and sadness. That's the problem with escapism. You may be able to remove yourself from the world for a few hours or even days, but the world keeps spinning. Life keeps happening.

By the fall of 2010, Issa, my father, Sally, and Malka were all dead. Joshua was in the sixth year of a twelve-year sentence for armed robbery and assault—a story I will tell in the final chapter—after being arrested on Mother's Day 2006. And in a few years—March of 2012—I would receive a judge's ruling that would determine the very meaning of Sally and Issa's love for me and all that they'd sacrificed. As the end of that year loomed, I'd committed to killing myself if the ruling went against me.

Issa used to tell me, "Mitchell, anytime you have the word *too* in it, that isn't any good. It doesn't matter if it's too big, too fast, too small, too much, too anything. It's no good. Everything in moderation."

Lee, the strip clubs, and massage parlors weren't tools to just escape my childhood wounds. I was trying to escape from life itself.

Life had and would continue to become too much.

Chapter 13
MOURNER'S *KADDISH*

WHEN RUSKA CALLED TO TELL US that Yosef had died, I felt the presence of death as a visceral truth for the first time in my life. That I believed I was the cause of Yosef's death added further emotional clarity to the youthful abstraction that death had been.

Death, I saw, has an eternality and finality to it that nothing else in life possesses.

And so, I knew that when Issa died, death would take my messiah from me. Ruska's call began an unabating fear for the day that Issa would die.

My childhood with Sally and Issa—my father present but a shadow—was happy, or at least, as happy as I could expect given all I'd been through. Like Sally and Issa did with their Holocaust experiences, I tamped my trauma down. It was one other way that I was like them.

Despite a few bumps here and there, the only moment of true conflict that ever interfered with our love for one another was that Betty was not Jewish. Once that was resolved, there was no more tension; everything went back to normal. I loved them, and they loved me.

With the return of normal came Issa's abundant and, at times, overwhelming financial support. He gave us forty thousand dollars to purchase our first house. Three years later, he gave us another hundred thousand dollars to buy a second, larger home that I would fanatically renovate. This became yet another addiction and means of escape that at times approached a mania. Issa also paid for Joshua's Montessori school and Hebrew summer camps. With this, Issa continually asked, "Does Joshua feel Jewish? Does he feel it in his soul? Does he really feel it?"

When I told them Betty and I were divorcing, they asked, "Why? She's a good girl." All I could say was that I couldn't be married to anyone.

My visits to them were regular and a pleasant routine, two times per week. More often than not, Issa would give me a "shot in the arm" of a few hundred, or sometimes a few thousand dollars. Each visit began with me—sometimes with Joshua and Betty—walking in the back door. "Is anybody home?" I'd call out.

"Everybody's home," Issa would reply in his Polish-inflected English. He'd either wake from what he called his "old man nap" or be at his desk working. "Everything okay?" he'd then ask.

"Yes, fine. I'm well."

"Do you need something?"

"No, I'm okay."

"What's new, Mitch? How's Joshua? How's the business?"

As much as I loved Sally, whenever I went to their home, it was to see Issa, who was semiretired by 1990. I'm not sure if this was something he chose or a negotiated settlement with Sally. With this change, he started doing more around the house. Occasionally, I'd arrive to see him at the sink doing the dishes. He was so gentle and calm in his mannerism standing there, an old man in suspenders, slacks, and shirt . . . this old teddy bear of a man doing dishes.

Sally was still the *balabusta* of the home, but she let Issa do the dishes because it obviously brought him pleasure.

One thing about Issa that hadn't changed was his insistence that his soup was hot. Not lukewarm or warm—HOT. There were so many meals I shared with them when Issa, often home after work, would dip his spoon into the soup, bring it to his lips, then drop the spoon into the bowl. "It's cold," he'd say as he slapped his hand on the table.

"It's good; it's okay," Sally would respond.

Issa would look at me like, *Can you believe it?* And I'd think, *What is wrong with Sally that she can't serve him a hot bowl of soup?* They had been married for fifty years. Issa was a simple man. He did not have fancy tastes in food or clothes. You could serve him almost anything, and he'd be happy to have it. But during the Holocaust, soup was a staple, and it was served one of two ways. If you were in good with the person with the ladle, they'd dip down deep into the pot to give you a more nourishing serving. Or they could skim the surface to give you the weakest broth.

When I was a kid and an adult, Issa liked to take us out to Junior's Delicatessen. We always had the same waitress, a woman who had worked there for twenty or thirty years. "What would you like?" she'd ask Issa.

As is polite, Issa always ordered last. He'd look at the waitress and say, "I would like corned beef extra lean, please, and I want a hot soup, and I want it hot like my women."

Sally would just look at me with disgust and embarrassment.

Issa would smile and chuckle like he was the funniest guy in the place.

He also always ordered tea, which would come with a tea bag in a teacup, hot water in a container on the side. When he wanted more, he'd say with one finger raised, "I want some hot water, but I would like it hot, please."

Issa also had the habit of reaching into his pants' pocket, his fingers searching the bottom of it. One day he told me he did that because in the labor camp in Russia, he'd do that hoping to find a crumb to put in his mouth; he was so cold and hungry. As he told me this story, he mimed the action then showed his pinched fingertips to me. "Not even a crumb,

Mitchell. I would put my hand in my pocket over and over, but there was never anything in it."

Of course, Sally had her own story, too, and had experienced the same if not worse than Issa. I also imagine that on the occasions she served warm or cool soup, perhaps that was her way of delivering a message of displeasure or anger to Issa. It would be the only instance that either of them shared annoyance with the other in front of me.

Issa also didn't like loud noises. If a customer came into his liquor store loud and drunk, Issa would say in a loud voice, "Be quiet. You'll wake up the baby!"

"What baby?" the person would invariably say. "There's no baby back there."

Issa would whisper, using his thickest Polish accent, "The baby. You'll wake it. Be quiet."

Before I left during many of my visits to Issa and Sally, he would ask once more, "Mitchell, do you need anything?"

"No. I'm fine."

Then he'd write a check for one thousand dollars.

"No, Issa, I don't want it . . . I don't need it."

He'd push it toward me, saying, "You need a shot in the arm. It's a shot in the arm."

I needed these shots in the arm more and more. I'd run out of money because of what I spent on my sexual addiction—and my other addiction, home renovations—and couldn't pay the mortgage. I was out of control. I'd visit Issa with my tail between my legs. I was dependent on him because business was slow and I'd spent my money on strippers. The more self-loathing I felt, the more I needed the escape of the strip clubs, then Lee. Within this, home renovations were also a poor and chaotic coping tool that I used to escape my unhappy marriage.

My visits to this man I loved more than any other person became tainted. I'd stand before him like a pathetic schmuck. "Do you need any-thing?" he'd ask.

And I'd lie to him about what was going on in my life. I came up with all sorts of cockamamie reasons why I needed three thousand here or two thousand there. I felt horrible, but I would take whatever Issa offered, or sometimes even ask for more. There were other times when I would say no even though I needed the money; I just couldn't bring myself to accept Issa's generosity.

If I went a few days without seeing him, he would miss me. For what-ever reason, he adored me. His love was always reassuring but also added to my sadness and depression because I felt terrible about what I was hid-ing and terrified he might find out. Invariably, if he hadn't seen me for a while, he'd call and leave a message: "I forgot my name, and I forgot my phone number. Please call me back."

I'd get home, listen to the message on the answering machine, but it would be late, and I was tired, so I wouldn't call him.

The next day, another message: "I forgot my name. I forgot my phone number. Mitch, please call me back. It's Issa. Please call me back. I'm wor-ried you are not calling me."

This was as much of a reprimand that I would ever receive from him. It was his nature to be humble and gentle.

I felt guilty and ashamed of myself, but it didn't stop me. I loved him dearly and didn't want our relationship to be about money, but I was being *that* person. When Betty and I divorced, Issa gave her seventy-five thousand dollars on top of the forty thousand and hundred thousand he'd previously given us to purchase our second home. Betty used that money to resettle herself. When she did that, I moved from my small, divorced-dad apartment back into the house we'd shared. But there were too many memories, and I still felt deep guilt about the affair and every-thing else, so I figured a change of context might help.

Issa didn't want me to sell the house. He begged me not to do it, but I told him it was too big, too much, too expensive. I also wanted to free myself from having to come to him for money. I figured that after selling the house, I'd have one hundred thousand dollars in my pocket.

When it sold, I raced to Issa and put a cashier's check with his name on it for one hundred thousand dollars right in front of him. I was proud beyond belief. Issa was devastated.

"Here, Mitchell. I don't want it." He handed the check back to me.

There was an awkward moment as I tried to understand what he was doing. I thought he'd be pleased and think I'd turned a corner. Instead, I'd hurt him. I'd never seen him so hurt.

"Issa, I want you to have this, to pay you back."

"No, Mitchell. I don't want it." He held the check as if I'd earned the money through some elicit means.

I was being selfish because I needed some form of redemption from my self-inflicted misery and deceit. But my messiah wanted me to accept his kindness as just that, kindness for me to have. I also came to realize that he'd been adamant that I not sell the house, and here I'd gone against his wishes and then presented him with the money. I'd thrown his generosity, his love for me, back in his face.

I hadn't comprehended what it meant to him. It killed me to see him so hurt.

We both acted as if that visit had never happened. Issa never held grudges. We'd had our moment of pain, and it was done. But I felt the pain of what I'd done for years. I have repeated nightmares about that house to this day.

This was Issa. Maybe two or three times I saw him raise his voice with Sally, which was testament to Issa's calm. Sally could be so unreasonable that it would drive you nuts. But Issa was one of a kind, a simple guy. Color blind, no sense of smell, a guy who was happy as long as the soup was hot. Never a boring man, but never an ego either. No need to prove anything. Just comfortable in his own skin. When he sat down to eat his breakfast, he chewed his toast loudly. I could hear him, but it wasn't rude or gross. It was savoring. I've never experienced that with anyone else, where I could vicariously relish something by listening to the manner in which he chewed and the enjoyment he derived from it.

In these moments, I'm sure he had some sort of memory muscle that reconnected him to the hundreds of times he dipped his fingers into his pockets and there was never a crumb.

◆ ◆ ◆

Beginning in 2000, Issa showed signs of Parkinson's and the initial stages of Alzheimer's. It did not help that his glaucoma was entering its later stages. A few years before, Sally asked me to take Issa's car keys from him. He'd taught me to drive when I was seventeen. Occasionally, Issa would cry out, "I'm losing my eyes . . . I cannot see." Whatever I said to try to help him feel better had no effect. As the Alzheimer's progressed, all I could do was listen since there was nothing I could do to ease his fear.

Alzheimer's is a progressive disease, and fortunately it did not advance with much speed at first. But as Issa's mind became cloudier, I realized that I had to step in to take on the daily responsibilities for him and Sally. I visited most days to sort through the mail for whatever checks that came in from his various investments and bank accounts. I made sure to deposit them, and I paid their bills. As with any true balabusta, Sally ran the home and Issa ran the business. Sally knew nothing of and had no part in any of Issa's paperwork or business dealings. She was clueless how much money they had in any of the banks they used and lost when it came to paying bills. She was more than happy when I stepped in, for us both. I was their son, and with Issa fading, this was happily my duty and responsibility toward them.

Early in his Alzheimer's, there were times when I'd visit to check on them to find Issa sitting at his desk working on this or that. He'd take his glasses off, place his hands over his eyes, and say, "Mitch, I'm not the same."

"I know, Issa, I know." We both knew what he was referring to. Validating his fear was the only solace I could offer.

In June 2004, about four years after the Alzheimer's diagnosis, Sally called me in a panic. "Mitch! I can't find Issa!"

"What? What do you mean?"

"I mean, I can't find Issa. We were about to take a walk when I said to him to wait while I put a sweater on. When I came back, he was gone."

"He's not anywhere outside?"

"No, Mitch. The door was open, and I looked, but nothing. Please, Mitch, come over. We must find him."

"Of course. I'm coming now. Wait for me."

I raced to their home, but by the time I got there, Sally had received a call from Cedar Sinai Hospital's emergency room. Issa had fallen crossing a street a few blocks from the house and had a large cut on his forehead. When I arrived at the ER, a nurse led me to an examination room where Issa was sitting up looking placid as a doctor sutured the large gash on his forehead. I had to turn my head from the sight of it.

After finishing, the doctor pulled me aside. "We found some abnormalities in his blood work that may be linked to cancer."

"Abnormalities?" I asked.

"He's severely anemic, and his CEA level is higher than normal. We'd like to do a CT scan."

The next day, a doctor told us that the CT scan and other tests confirmed that Issa had stage IV metastatic colon cancer. The doctor laid out the options: surgery and chemo—he might not survive the operation, the doctor said—or home with hospice care. The news was devastating. I delivered the news to Sally and asked what she thought we should do.

"Oh, Mitch," she cried. "I don't know; I don't."

"We should tell Issa and see what he has to say," I told her. She agreed.

I sat with Issa, and choking on my tears, I told him the diagnosis and the options. Then I told him a cure was not possible, just maybe more time with the surgery and chemo, but he might not survive either.

Issa turned his head from me. "I don't know. You decide."

There wasn't an option to save Issa's life. There was only one option. Pain. Parkinson's, Alzheimer's, and glaucoma had already dimmed and diminished his life. At age eighty-six, Issa was a dying man. If we couldn't give him more life, we could give him as comfortable and dignified a death as possible in his home. So that's what Sally and I chose for him.

Sally was nine years older than Issa, and at age ninety-five, she was emotionally and physically bereft of the ability to provide any care for Issa. As you may have noticed, I have not mentioned my father much. He was present, but his pains and fear made his life small. Like Sally, he hovered about but could offer nothing in terms of support.

So, as Sally and Issa's son-in-name-only, Sally gave me the permission, trust, and confidence to make all decisions regarding Issa's care as well as anything else pertaining to their lives. For so much of my life, Issa had cared for me, and Sally in her own, sometimes exasperating way had been the only true mother I'd ever known, so now it was my time to care for them. And I did.

At the same time, Lee and my related addictions and dependencies were still firing on all cylinders. Picture me as your next-door neighbor. He's a stand-up guy and well-mannered. Works hard. Takes diligent care of his elderly parents. Divorced but by all appearances, an engaged father with a strong co-parenting relationship with his ex-wife. The ex-wife even invites him over to dinner on occasion. He seems normal, maybe even righteous, and yet he was a drug user, abuser of alcohol, and a sex addict engaged in a tumultuous affair.

For me, life was all about binging. All in as a parent. All in as an HVAC businessowner. All in as the custodian to my elderly parents. But also, all in on my addictions. On the nights I had no other responsibilities, I was out of control.

The reason all these compartments never collided into one another, causing my entire life to fall apart, was that I was a functioning addict. I hurt physically and emotionally, I was deeply depressed and anxiety-filled, and I held in a massive load of self-loathing . . . but even as I faced the thing that terrified me the most throughout my life—losing Issa—I functioned.

♦ ♦ ♦

Soon after Issa's diagnosis, while at the house helping with some paperwork and visiting Issa, there was a knock on the door. When Sally answered it, in walked my Aunt Yetty—she married Uncle Joe, Sally and my father's brother—and her two kids, my cousins Boris and Toby. Yetty's husband had died in the early 1970s, and Issa had been something of a financial savior to them. With Issa in his final months, Yetty and my cousins arrived, promising to become a much bigger presence in Sally and Issa's lives.

As if we didn't already have enough to deal with.

♦ ♦ ♦

By the fall of 2004, it was certain that Issa would soon die. Each day he seemed to slip a little further away. Whether it was the Alzheimer's or cancer that produced each day's deterioration, I don't know, but as he neared his final day, Issa—the person, the man I loved more than any other, my hero—was a vanishing figure. I did everything I could with the help of caretakers and hospice to ensure he was comfortable and make sure that Sally felt secure in her home and finances. But the fear and anxiety I'd carried for more than twenty-five years about how I would cope once Issa was gone was finally too much.

That's when I found Ann.

I sat in her office, a classic if not stereotypical therapist's office, and told her about Issa and Sally and me. I explained in detail all that I'd done over the past few months to care for them, how proud I was to take on that responsibility, that it was hard but good work, and how I was overwhelmed by the thought of losing Issa.

I told her that as far back as I could remember, Issa had always been there for me in one way or another. From my early childhood years, I looked up to him as my hero. As I became a young adult, he was my sweet, loving, and caring uncle. Between Sally and my father, Issa was the best, most liberal, and most open to giving me my freedom. Issa was the one who said I should have a bike when I was a boy. Issa was the one who taught me how to drive a car and then offered to buy me my first car.

But it wasn't about what he was willing to buy me. It was what he wanted me to feel; he wanted me to feel okay with life. He always wanted me to feel safe and know that he and Sally loved me more than if I had been their biological son. His love was the most unconditional love and devoted love I had ever known. The list of events and things he had done through my life was, and is, priceless.

Issa used to tell me how his own father beat him all the time. He would get spanked and beaten by his old man for no apparent reason. He told me on many occasions, "I would be standing next to my father, and he would look down at me and start to hit me. Hit me for no reason. And he'd hit my mother, too. One day, when I was a teenager, I stepped between my father and mother as he was beating her, and I told him,

'From now on, you are no longer going to hit Mother.' And that was the last time he did."

Issa never spanked or hit me. There were at least a couple times when he certainly had a good reason to, but he never did. I tried very hard to be respectful and polite as much as a child can be. Feeling like I was practically adopted by them or rescued like some sort of abused animal from my mother, I never felt at liberty to be a brat or difficult child. I always felt so grateful to have Sally and Issa in my life, ever since I could remember. I do not know if I would have had the will to go on with life if it weren't for Sally and Issa coming to the rescue, taking me away from life with my mother.

Starting when I was in my mid-twenties, I had fearful thoughts of Issa dying and leaving me alone. I knew he was getting older, and the day would certainly come when he would die. I was married to Betty at the time, and many times when the phone rang, it sent a shock of fear up my spine. *What if . . .* I'd think. The older I got, the more I hoped he would live to a point where I felt I had reached a level of maturity and responsibility that I would be able to manage my own life without having to rely on Issa as my safety net.

You see, I told Ann, Issa was always there to clean up my messes. Most of them were financial. What scared me the most over the past twenty-five years was how could I trust myself to do the right things in life. I knew that once Issa was gone, there wouldn't be anyone else to look after me. No more safety net. No more hero to rescue me. When Issa was dead, would I lose my mind? Would I crumble? Would I be frivolous and run everything into the ground?

And so, I explained to Ann how afraid I was to lose the one person who had looked after me my whole life. Would I be capable of managing without him, and was I ready?

In her notes from that first session, which she later shared with me, Ann wrote:

Mitchell shared many symptoms of a person in a deep state of acute anxiety. I immediately identified that he suffers from severe impacts from his childhood experiences and losses. I gave him a safe space to talk about mistreatment by his mother and about the people he needed to count on for stability and support. This was a man who had been tossed around, had no stability except for when his aunt and uncle adopted him. Mitch is a man who presents as all together and caring and there for others, but inside is deeply troubled and unable to establish a truly meaningful relationship with anyone. He is a poser: presenting as a man all together but deeply troubled.

It would be a few more weeks before Ann deployed the well-dressed poser line, but already she'd seen it.

After I spoke, Ann allowed a silence to settle between us. Her lips formed a wan smile, like she knew the one thing I didn't. "Mitch, you are already doing the thing you've most feared you would never be able to do. You have *already* been managing everything for Issa, Sally, and your son for the last few months."

It took Ann only a few seconds and one simple sentence to obliterate twenty-five years of me living with the self-doubt over how I would carry on after Issa passed. I knew right away I had stumbled upon a guide I would allow to counsel and comfort me for years to come. Ann became an essential person helping me to understand how to handle the present crisis and how my past and my family's past had shaped who I'd become.

As with any good-to-great addict, the will to keep the addiction was strong. I still had another seven years to go. But for the first time, the tips of my toes brushed the ground.

◆ ◆ ◆

On February 9, 2005, Issa died.

On February 11, I buried my messiah and hero.

During the last eight months of his life, not once did Issa utter a word of self-pity. I was so proud of his valor. Sally, on the other hand, was a different story. Sally felt that she was the victim and became angry at Issa for dying and leaving her. She would now look upward and say, "Why did you do this to me?"

Sally cried every day for the next five years. "I can't help myself from crying," she would say.

Meanwhile, it felt as if Yetty, Boris, and Toby had taken up residence in Sally and Issa's home, as close to Sally's ear and checkbook as possible.

◆ ◆ ◆

I continued to see Ann. We talked about my childhood, my dependency toward Lee, my struggles trying to take care of Sally, the balancing act of family members trying to influence Sally to give them money, my relationship with Malka that was one of love and frustration but also happiness as she found her way, and much more.

In March 2006, Sally called to tell me that my father had been admitted to Kaiser hospital. He'd been home in his tiny apartment eating a sandwich and a piece of it lodged in his throat. He was able to clear his throat but not completely, and because of that, he developed pneumonia that progressed to the point that he required hospitalization and a ventilator. For the next month, he was hospitalized and bedridden with a ventilator tube down his throat.

Sally and I visited as often as we could. They were brief, sad visits. Eventually, the doctor discharged him to a convalescent home. He was still extremely weary, fragile, and uncomfortable, which also made each visit difficult.

Not even two weeks after the transfer—April 29, 2006—I went to visit my father late one afternoon. He was asleep, so I decided to leave. As I walked out of the room, I heard, "Come back! Don't leave! Please!"

"I have to go," I said. "I have an appointment with Ann. Get some sleep. I'll be back."

Then I left.

At about 6:20 p.m.—just after leaving my session with Ann—my phone rang. I was tired, hungry, emotionally drained. Traffic was heavy, and I was getting nowhere. "Hello?"

"Is this Mr. Raff?"

"Yes, speaking."

"This is Jan from the convalescent home. I'm calling to inform you that your father just passed away."

"Okay, thank you for the call. I'll come by tomorrow." I ended the call, and my thoughts went back to the traffic.

A minute went by. Then I began to question what just happened. *Did I just get a call saying my dad died, or am I starting to imagine things?*

I picked up the phone and redialed the number. The same voice answered.

"This is Mitchell Raff calling. Did you just call me and tell me that my father died?"

"Yes. Yes, I did."

It was no longer my imagination or my mind playing tricks on me. My mind and body became numb. The traffic was no longer an issue. The next day, I went back to the convalescent home to sign the paperwork and pick up my dad's personal items.

His passing was as simple as that. Dachau never let go of him, and he never let go of it. It ruined his life and his ability to be a father to me, so I believe that I've been mourning his loss my entire life. At first, it was an ambiguous sense of loss and mourning, but with his death, the loss was palpable.

With Dad's death, the monthly compensation checks from Germany for his time in Dachau ended. I've always wondered if he found the money comforting or a monthly reminder of the horror.

As of October 2022, Germany for more than seventy years had paid eighty billion euros to survivors. It's hard to imagine putting a monetary price on the Holocaust, but there it is.

◆ ◆ ◆

In 2007, Ruska was the next to go. She died of old age surrounded by an adoring family. She was a rare and lovely woman.

Meanwhile, back in Los Angeles, Aunt Yetty and the cousins were up to no good. Of course, I had some idea of what they were up to but not the complete picture. I also knew that Issa and Sally had helped Uncle Joe and his family financially from time to time.

After the Holocaust, Joe emigrated to Los Angeles and became a finish carpenter and cabinetmaker, though he never managed to achieve much success. When Issa opened one of his liquor stores—in the mid-1960s—he brought Joe in to help him run it. Both men and their respective families were close; they only lived about ten miles apart. Then in the early 1970s, around the time Issa rescued me from Mother, Joe was diagnosed with kidney cancer. It only took six months for him to die. Afterward, Sally visited Yetty quite often, and there were numerous holidays and dinners spent with Yetty and the cousins. Issa and Sally would sit in the kitchen with Yetty happily talking and gossiping about family and friends. Issa also felt bad for Yetty and her children, so he started helping them out financially.

Rather than feeling grateful, Yetty took on the attitude of the aggrieved widow, a bitter woman who felt deprived and cheated by life. She was also likely quite jealous of all that Sally and Issa had. And though my memories of Uncle Joe are scant, I remember him as rather cold. Not so much unfriendly, just not a warm person. With him gone and Yetty's bitterness increasing, she raised her children to be bitter and cold as well, as if the world owed them so much more than they had.

Issa's financial assistance helped Boris and Toby attend UCLA, after which they married and basically lived their lives. But they never stopped hitting Issa up for money. Yetty worked as a seamstress, the same career as Ruska, and probably received regular help from Issa, too. So, we interacted with each other with some frequency, even though we didn't particularly like one another.

After Issa died, Yetty and the cousins visited with Sally more frequently, often bringing their young children to sweeten Sally up and get her to feel more connected to them. Yetty had raised the cousins to know that Sally and Issa had quite a bit of wealth and to behave in ways that ensured they would be part of the inheritance. Their efforts increased with Issa gone. The three of them took turns visiting Sally with the goal of creating the impression that they simply wanted to support and console her.

I found it annoying and worried about their constant visits and fawning over Sally, but I was unaware that they were becoming more brazen in their manipulative behaviors. They bad-mouthed me to Sally, saying I was taking advantage of her. They also started to ply her for more and more money. At first it was relatively small amounts that grew to include enough money to buy an apartment building. They claimed poverty or ill health were the reasons they needed so much support, but of course the cousins were far more financially secure than they let on. Toby, for example, was divorced and living in a two-million-dollar home in Beverly Hills bought by her ex-husband, a trial lawyer named Stephen.

Throughout this time, I was taking care of all the bills, incoming finances, home needs, health needs, and on and on for Sally while Yetty and the cousins would visit, usually leaving with a check. I remember writing many of these checks for fifteen or twenty-five thousand dollars after Sally implored me to help them. I would gently question the wisdom of giving them so much, but at the same time, it was Sally's money.

One day, while visiting Sally, she told me that Boris needed financial help. His struggles were too much, so she wanted to give him the small strip mall that he was supposed to inherit after Sally passed. "He could benefit from the monthly income now," she told me.

It was obvious that Yetty or Boris, or both, put this idea into her head, but I said, "Yes, Sally, that's a good idea." I thought to myself, *Yes, let's give him the strip mall now instead of waiting until you die so you can stop worrying about poor, sick Boris and his supposed financial woes.*

Once, after driving to her house to give Yetty yet another check—this one for forty thousand dollars—she said, "You think this makes it right? You think this makes up for anything?" I had no idea what wrongs Sally or I were supposed to make up to her, Boris, and Toby. Her jealousy and resentment were formidable.

Other times, I'd visit Sally, and one of her caretakers would pull me aside. "The cousins came again with Yetty and said terrible things about you to Sally."

"Such as?"

"How you're taking advantage of her, that she shouldn't trust you, that sort of thing."

"The usual?"

"Yes. The usual."

When I'd see Sally, she'd be crying and in a bad mood, then tell me it was Yetty and/or the cousins that caused it.

"These are lies," I'd tell Sally. "They want to manipulate you." But because of how aggressive they were and the pressure they put on her—as well as her advanced age—it was difficult for Sally to know what was true. She cried every single day for Issa, for her brother's death, for Ruska's death, for Joshua's horrible crimes and incarceration, for the life she now led. She was miserable and beaten down, afraid. Every day, she'd sob, "Why are you doing this to me, Issa? Why is this happening to me? Mitch, I can't help it . . . I can't." She was lost and could not see what was happening.

This is how Sally spent the last five years of her life—traumatized by the death of her beloved Issa and tormented and harassed by Yetty and the cousins. What they did was disgusting and morally corrupt. I remember my father as far back as I can remember telling me that Yetty was a terrible person. Soon after Issa died, he said, "She's causing harm to you and Sally. I hate that woman."

The worst was to come.

◆ ◆ ◆

It was November 2008, the Sunday before Thanksgiving. That morning Malka left her apartment to run some errands. She drove her car to the first stop sign on her street, only about twenty feet from her home. There was a parked car to her left that created a blind spot for her as she got ready to make a left onto Oxnard Boulevard.

She made the turn, not realizing there was a jeep racing down Oxnard. The jeep collided with Malka at full speed. My sister was brain dead upon impact. A week later, on November 21, I allowed the doctors to take her off life support. She died that night.

Her last words to me were in a phone message the Friday before to wish me a good Shabbat. "Mitchell, this is your sister. If you want to call me, you have to do it before 5:45 p.m. tonight. I love you very, very, very much." After all we'd been through as brother and sister, after all she'd been through, there are no words to describe what her message meant and continues to mean to me. I first saw her and fell in love with her when I was four years old; Mother had just screamed at my father who pliantly walked away, and I looked into the bright-eyed, beautiful face of the sister I'd never met. Malka, I love you too, very, very much.

The following Sunday, I flew with Malka's body to Israel to see her buried in an orthodox Jewish cemetery in Jerusalem, a city she loved dearly. Staring at Malka's newly dug grave, I felt numb, still in a state of shock and not really able to process the meaning of her sudden death. Five days later, a cab drove me back to the cemetery for one last goodbye. As I walked from my sister's grave, I felt a wrenching separation so powerful that my knees buckled.

◆ ◆ ◆

Sally had always been fastidious in her appearance. Even well into her nineties, she did her makeup and hair and dressed in fashionable clothes. When she stopped caring for her appearance, I knew the end was near.

Home care was no longer enough, so I decided to place her in an assisted living facility. When I informed Toby, she said, "Yes, Mitch, we've done all we can."

Her words were a pathetic joke and a slap in the face. The truth was that my cousins and their mother hadn't done anything other than torment and emotionally abuse her for the past five years.

I visited Sally in the facility the day we moved her. I can't remember the last time I had been so tense and nervous to see her. I didn't want to betray her by taking her from her home, by undermining the proud and vain woman I'd known since childhood. *She'll kill me for this*, I thought. But when I arrived, she didn't seem particularly aware of her circumstances. She recognized me instantly, and her face lit up with a toothless smile. She was happy to see me, and I'd never felt so lifted by her smile.

Two weeks later, June 9, 2010, at age ninety-nine and a half, Sally suffered heart failure. She died before I could reach her.

Thus ended a string of deaths, the sadness and sense of loss I've not yet recovered from:

- Issa in 2005

- My father in 2006

- Ruska in 2007

- Malka in 2008

- Sonya, a dear friend, in 2009

- Sally in 2010

I was now truly an orphan.

I was also in many respects a father without his child. Just a month after my father died, Joshua was arrested. About a year after that, he was sentenced to twelve years in prison. Though his loss was not a death, it was an ambiguous loss that removed him from my life, one that required its own path of mourning. For five years, I felt his loss when I woke and then again as I lay down for sleep. Those who've experienced the incarceration of a loved one, especially a son or daughter, will know exactly what I mean. Those left behind, on the outside, also feel a vicarious sense of imprisonment.

And so, with Sally's death—the last of my six parents—I was truly an orphan, once again alone in the world.

◆ ◆ ◆

Robert, an attorney, started dating Toby in 1998, eventually moving in with her in her house. After about five or six years, Toby discovered that Robert was cheating on her, which ended their relationship. For the five years prior to Sally's death, Robert was our acting lawyer helping manage Sally and Issa's financial and legal affairs. I'd hired him when I stopped using Issa's original law firm because they were too expensive and rarely returned my calls. I believed I could trust Robert to have our best interests at heart in representing the estate.

I also knew Issa and Sally's will by heart.

So, a few weeks after Sally's death, I stood in Robert's office ready to execute the final wishes of Sally and Issa. With the exception of nine family members receiving an equal cash inheritance of fifty thousand dollars each, I would inherit the little money that was left of the estate plus a shopping center of my own. Toby got Sally and Issa's house and was one of the nine to receive fifty thousand dollars. Boris would also get fifty thousand dollars and had already received his strip mall.

Robert walked into his office to an oval conference table where I stood waiting for him. Before saying a word—not even a word of condolence for Sally—I noticed his fingertips slide two pieces of paper toward me. I looked at the papers. "What's this?"

"Sally amended the will back in 2007." His eyes were smug, his voice conniving.

The amendment said that I would share my inheritance four ways between Boris, Toby, and Lea, a cousin in Israel. Stricken, I looked at Robert.

"Should you decide to contest this amendment and lose in court, according to the terms of the will, you will lose your entire inheritance."

"Robert," I said, "I'm surprised you didn't arrange for security to be here."

"My secretary said I should have."

"You should've listened to her. I'm not a violent man, otherwise, I would be throwing you out that window right now." His office was on the nineteenth floor with an all-glass exterior wall that overlooked a golf course in the distance.

He then told me that Sally had come to his office in 2007 with the help of Toby. After forty-five minutes, they "persuaded" Sally to sign the amendment without speaking a word of it to me. Not only was this kept secret for three years, but I was a trustee of Issa's estate. The law required them to inform me.

I looked at Robert. "I'll be hiring one hell of a lawyer, and I'll be seeing you in court."

I hired two lawyers: one to represent me and the other to represent me as a trustee. A little more than a year later—November 2011—I had my day in court. In one of the first meetings with my lawyers, they made it very clear what the stakes were: The judge had to void the amendment in its entirety. Anything less than that, and I would lose my case, the cousins and Yetty would have the right to countersue me, and they could remove me as a trustee. It would bankrupt me financially and spiritually.

The money meant far less than the potential loss of my identity, of what I meant to Sally and Issa and what they meant to me. I was fighting for my right to be their son, to honor the sacrifices and time and love that Sally and Issa had made for me. I was fighting to give meaning to the moment Sally turned to see the saddened toddler and stopped Issa, saying, "We can't leave him," to Issa finding me walking to school and noticing the bruises and welts caused by my mother's physical abuse, to her escape with Malka and me to Israel to . . . to everything these two wonderful people did for me.

And I was fighting the abuse of Sally, an elderly and bereft woman, by Yetty, Boris, and Toby. Evil must not prevail. I had to fight, no matter the outcome.

During the legal period of discovery when depositions and other facts of the case were collected, I learned that the amendment had been prepared prior to the office meeting with Sally in 2007 by Robert—her estate lawyer—based on information provided by Toby and Boris, the two people who would benefit the most. I also learned that Toby and Robert took the amendment to Sally's house to have her sign it, but she refused. According to Robert's deposition, Sally refused to sign it in part because she was scared that I would find out. The office meeting happened a few days later with Toby driving Sally to Robert's office to pressure her to sign the amendment for a second time. Again, Sally refused, but they kept her there for almost an hour until she caved.

All this for an amendment Sally supposedly wanted and had asked for. The fact was that they terrorized a ninety-six-year-old woman into signing the amendment. Toby, Boris, and Yetty, with Robert's help, preyed on an elderly woman.

Over the year of preparing for court, the thought of losing this battle consumed me and dragged me as far down as I'd ever been in my life. I reached a place where if I should lose, suicide was unquestioned, but perhaps, too, was taking the lives of the people causing so much harm to Sally and Issa, their memory and legacy. The mind in such circumstances can conjure all manner of darkness. Mine was no different.

We had our day in court—days, actually. Made our arguments. The other side made theirs. The correct result seemed clear to me, but the law on this issue gave an advantage to Yetty and the cousins. Despite their hectoring and manipulation, Sally had signed the amendment. There was also no document declaring that Sally and Issa had adopted me. Despite Issa and Sally saving me from the orphanage and all they did to rescue me from my mother and raise me, I was just another nephew in the eyes of the court. There was no telling what the judge would decide.

Anything was possible.

◆ ◆ ◆

Since ending my affair with antidepressants, I'd worked on strategies to resist by force of will my frequent descents into depression and anxiety. Did this really work? Not really. After Florence, I had moved past my need for strip clubs but not the perverse need for Lee.

With the battle over Issa and Sally's legacy—truly, the meaning of my entire life—consuming me emotionally, I needed an escape more than ever. Lee was the means for everything to stop for a few hours. It was December 2011—after the final hearing before the judge in November—when Lee called. "How are you? I miss you . . ." And thus, our cycle of sex and breakups began once more.

In another perverse twist, the expense of the lawyers forced me to sell my home. With no other option and a kind offer, I moved in with Betty. One last small irony is that Issa had given her the money to purchase her house after our divorce.

For this reason, when Lee and I arranged to have one of our "sessions" on New Year's Eve 2011, there was no choice but to book a hotel room.

As we walked into the hotel room that night, I was tired. I was tired of her, tired of needing her, tired of living in a constant state of overwhelm and hypervigilance, tired of not having Issa in my life, tired of abusing drugs and alcohol, tired of hating myself. As good and helpful and wonderful as Ann was, she was no match for my need for whatever it was that Lee provided. I had reached a point where walking into that hotel room with Lee was like finally giving in to my addiction, to accepting that my addiction eventually would kill me. *Bring it on*, I thought as a final capitulation.

Do I blame Lee for it all? No. I blame myself, too. Responsibility goes both ways.

I mixed a drink—cranberry and vodka—and dropped a bit of meth into it, took a sip. Like a well-worn groove, I threw a verbal jab at her. "You know what? Leave me alone. I'm taking a bath to chill out. I need some time alone."

Lee wasn't happy, and she was high on meth. She watched me walk into the bathroom where I ran water, took my clothes off, then climbed into the tub. A minute later, Lee came in. Rather than join me, she stood above me and eased into her usual airing of grievances with me: all the reasons I'd failed her, all the reasons why she deserved better, all the reasons I was such a fuck-up and fucking up her life. It was a type of torture that she'd perfected over the years—I had my own tortures for her, to be sure—and in that moment, something snapped.

I stood in the tub, milky water halfway up my shins. "I am so done with you," I said. "I am so done with all of this shit. I am done with using drugs. I am done with everything."

She started screaming at me, "You're done? Fuck you! I'm done!"

I pushed past her, dried myself off, and dressed while she continued shouting. When she realized I was serious, that I was leaving, she put her body between me and the door leading to the hall.

"Out of the way!" I yelled.

She dug in deeper. She screamed at me not to leave, then shifted from rage to pleading like a little girl not getting her way. I screamed back at her. It was a shouting match and a physical struggle. I became desperate to get out of that room, to run away. She was desperate to force me to stay, to talk it out. With her high on meth, I knew she could not and would not stop talking. She could go for hours, an entire day. I couldn't take it, not again. No more. I was angry and disgusted with myself for my immoral behavior, for being so weak, for all the drug use and drinking, for every poor decision, for letting this pathetic scene play out for the thousandth time.

I shoved her aside and left the room at a trot and soon broke into a sprint to escape her. I headed to the stairway—the elevator would take too long, be too passive; I needed to run. When I finally burst through the front doors of the hotel into the cool Los Angeles air, I breathed deeply over and over, feeling the oxygen hit my lungs, its winter moistness against my skin.

◆ ◆ ◆

In many recovery programs—especially Alcoholics Anonymous and Narcotics Anonymous—they speak of a moment of awakening. This was mine. There is no other explanation why in that moment I found the will and strength to leave. After decades of abusing drugs and alcohol, sexual addiction, and addiction to Lee and all that she meant, the failures and damage in my life piling up, I was able to enter lasting recovery. It was a moment of clarity when I decided I couldn't live like this anymore. That night ended my drug use. Nothing since. It was the last time I drank like an alcoholic. By some miracle, I had not become addicted to alcohol, and once the emotional dependence was excised, so too was any need to abuse alcohol.

It was also the last time I ever saw Lee. I was no longer bound by a codependent addiction to whatever the sum of us was.

◆ ◆ ◆

On March 12, 2012, after a year and nine months of wondering whether I would live or die, the judge finally delivered his lengthy verdict in court. He noted that had the circumstances been even a little different, his ruling would have been much different. His tone was chatty, to the point of informal, saying that both sides were well-represented. I had no idea where he was going with any of this, but then he noted Robert's relationship with Toby, his lack of professionalism for continuing to represent the trust, and how he had engineered the amendment to the benefit of his former lover. The judge seemed miffed by this.

Finally, he stated, "I am hereby declaring that the 2007 amendment is invalid."

May, one of my lawyers, said she heard Toby crying.

In an addendum to his ruling, the judge wrote, "Upon rereading the trial transcripts and reviewing all of the documentary evidence, the Court further finds that the procurement of the August 10, 2007, trust amendment was the direct product of undue influence and duress . . ."

I waited anxiously for the sixty-day period within which they could file an appeal to expire, and then immediately sued Toby, Boris, and

Robert for my trustee legal fees. We agreed to mediation, and I once again won another legal battle worth $275,000 for legal expenses.

Despite Sally and Issa never adopting me—a gesture of respect to my father—I was now truly and fully their son.

Joshua still had five more years on his prison sentence to serve. I hoped for him to have his own moment of personal awakening before it was too late. It never came.

◆ ◆ ◆

A coda:

In August 2022 my lawyer May called. "May, why are you calling me?"

"Hi, Mitch—"

"No, May. Why are you calling me?"

"I need to tell you something because I need to know if you're okay with this. I got a call from Stephen—"

"Toby's ex-husband?"

"Yes. And he dropped the name Robert while we were speaking . . ."

Robert, of course, was Toby's former live-in boyfriend who shared her multi-million-dollar Beverly Hills house that Stephen—also a lawyer—bought when he was married to Toby. And Robert was the same attorney I hired and trusted to help manage Sally's estate who then betrayed Sally and me by helping Toby and Boris abuse and pressure Sally into signing the amendment to her will in his office.

Stephen's law partner referred him to May, completely unaware of our history.

". . . I just wanted to know if it's okay with you if I take the case."

May went on to explain that Toby had died four years prior—no one had told me—and that Yetty had died a month before. Yetty was a Holocaust survivor herself. Toby would get frantic calls from her mother, who would cry and express her fears that the Nazis were trying to break into her house. Yetty was diagnosed with dementia, and while slowly deteriorating and dying, Boris pulled the same stunt on her that he and Toby pulled on Sally. Yetty's illness gave Boris years to apply his undue influence on his mother. He had Yetty amend her will behind everyone's back to exclude Toby's children—the children she had with her ex-husband, Stephen—from Yetty's estate. Despite Yetty's whining about money and constant pleas to Sally for more money, her estate, I believe, was worth two to three million dollars.

"So, Stephen says he needs a lawyer for his kids to fight Boris." May started to laugh. "When Stephen found out who I am, he said, 'Oh, you're the one.'"

"I'm floored," I said. "Of course it's okay. Just make sure my name is in the transcripts. I don't care how you reference me, but I want my name somewhere in this lawsuit as a reference to my own lawsuit to show that this is a pattern Boris has."

Chapter 14

JOSHUA

DESPITE ALL THE PAIN AND INSANITY of his father, Joshua was born into love.

Betty and I loved him dearly and had every hope for his happiness. Issa and Sally, my father, too, as well as Malka . . . everyone who knew and loved me loved Joshua.

The same was true of Betty's family, a huge collection of brothers and sisters—five boys and five girls—with their own large mass of children and extended family.

The number of people who loved Joshua from the moment of his birth was impressive.

But he grew up with me, a father with one foot in another secret world defined by addiction and addictive behavior. My entire life I believed I could reject the doom and gloom with which Sally and Issa naturally looked at history, and sometimes, life. I didn't want to inherit the damage that my mother's past had done to her. Sometimes, though, you don't get to choose what you inherit. You just create another persona to protect you from it and present that person to the world. But the faults, fears, insecurities, impulsivity, and so on never disappear. They are always present to affect the life of the person they possess. Ergo the well-dressed poser.

And so, at a young age, Joshua found himself the only child of a divorced couple. His mother had her faults, but it was his father who knew for three years that he was too broken to be married . . . to anyone.

It is cliché to say but nonetheless true that divorce is never easy for the children. The parents escape something that made at least one, if not both, desperately unhappy. In doing so, they make their children desperately unhappy. It is the saddest truth of divorce that as parents, we all would do anything for our children's safety and happiness. We would lay down our own lives without hesitation. And yet, returning to our children's other parent is the one thing that they want most, but it is the one thing as parents we cannot do.

Joshua didn't grow up in a household with abuse and fights. For him, it was relatively normal and peaceful. I was never drunk or high when he was with me. I never exposed him to any of the bad, acting-out behaviors I indulged in. He met and knew Lee—which was bad enough—but the crazy never came out around him.

Yet I am well aware that children have a finely tuned radar for their parent's behavior, seen and unseen. Perhaps (probably?) Joshua knew more than he let on. Perhaps (probably?) he'd had his feelings and emotional well-being harmed far more than I was aware of by choices I made that I believed were beyond his line of sight. Perhaps (probably?) in his own way, he knew from an early age that I was a well-dressed poser, even if he didn't know the specifics.

I must take ownership of these things, and I do.

But he also went to Montessori and other good schools. Despite our divorce, Betty and I remained committed to co-parenting Joshua with love and to building a friendship between the two of us for Joshua to plainly see. He went to summer camps of all sorts—not just Jewish-oriented—he loved sports, had Gameboys and loved Pokémon (was practically a video game addict), had friends, lived with financial security, and had the undying emotional and financial support of Issa and other extended family.

He was diagnosed with ADHD—like me—at an early age, so he took medication, but was in nearly every respect, a normal and abundantly loved child.

But there were the wounds passed from one generation to the next that began with the Holocaust. It's not an excuse but rather a truth, a fact of Joshua's inheritance. Had I been healthier emotionally, Joshua may not have been an only—and lonely—child of divorce. Furthermore, he was a latchkey kid. Betty worked with a long commute, and I continued to work a huge number of hours each week. So, there he was, a sad and lonely middle school kid waking up and getting ready for school alone, walking to school alone, feeling like an outsider at school, then coming home to an empty house. He needed to find his tribe. This was and remains one of my biggest regrets.

At age fifteen, he started to act out. It was as though he'd flipped a switch. He was too young to perfect the ability to compartmentalize the pieces of his life, to play the role of the well-dressed poser. His most profound instantiation was what I call an identity crisis. He embraced the violent imagery of gangster rap and took that on as his persona to protect himself from his internalized pains. I can see why. It offered rebellion that hurt his mother and me while offering instant identity and connection with other kids his age equally as lost and in pain.

I told him he looked like an idiot with the huge, baggy pants and other affectations of the gangster rappers with whom he started to identify. "You are not a gangster rapper, so stop pretending to be one," I said.

I asked Betty if she was experiencing the same behaviors in her home. She said yes.

"Joshua, you are acting stupid," I told him. "And your friends are laughing behind your back."

When I saw him a week or two later, he'd adopted the persona of a Chicano gang member. Since Joshua was part Peruvian from Betty's father, he had a little bit of a Hispanic look to him.

This was a time—2001 time frame—when adopting the persona of gangster rap was incredibly seductive to certain groups of kids. It was a stereotype—an offensive one, to be sure—but it captured them in the same way that the hippie look and aesthetic, as well as the drugs, captured many of my generation. For quite a few of both generations, the persona became lifelong. And for both, it was a huge negative attention grab. The power lives in how it speaks to kids—of any race, family, ethnicity—who are lonely, who feel like outsiders, who don't believe they have another cultural home. It validates them, fills a hole within their lives, and gives them a sense of self and belonging.

And it annoys and scares the shit out of their parents, the people whom many of them blame for their unhappiness and lack of belonging.

For Joshua, he found belonging in a toxic culture that fed his anger and hurt.

Before long, he stopped living with me, choosing to be with his mother. Then one night, I received a panicked call from Betty. "Joshua's gone missing!"

We called the police, checked hospitals, called his friends, did all we could to find him. It was the first big test of his independence and his power, or lack of power.

Joshua came home, but as the days and weeks passed, his acting out became worse. Truancy became routine, as did stealing, fighting, drinking, using drugs, and probably a whole lot more I'm not aware of. Betty and I did what we could, including sending him to a Scared Straight program. He laughed at the police counselors and their stories of what would happen to him if he continued down his current path.

In his final year of high school, Joshua stole a box of blank checks from a neighbor's mailbox, then was arrested trying to cash one that he'd forged. When he and I went to court over this, I hoped that finally he'd receive a severe enough punishment to wake him up. He'd already learned that his mother and I would not physically fight him, nor could we control his behavior. He was making his own choices, so hopefully with some accountability he'd choose a better life for himself.

Joshua received probation and a sternly worded warning from the judge. It was less than a slap on the wrist; he wouldn't even have to pick up trash on the roadside.

"Excuse me, Your Honor!" I called out.

"And who may you be?" the judge asked.

"I'm his father, and I have to tell you, I fear for his life."

"Oh?" the judge said.

"I fear that he's a danger to himself, to others."

The judge considered what I'd said for a moment. Joshua glared at me.

"Well," began the judge, "if that's the case, I hereby sentence Joshua Raff to four months in juvenile detention camp."

Joshua whispered, "You're an asshole."

For the first time in years, I believed Joshua would get what he needed. I walked out of the courthouse feeling a slight sense of victory.

That feeling was short-lived.

Joshua emerged from juvie unrepentant, unrehabilitated, and more dedicated to his self-destructive friends—his new family—and lifestyle.

About a year before—when he was sixteen—after an incident at school, Joshua saw a psychologist, which did not last long and had no effect. After his last session, the psychologist pulled me aside. "Your son will get in trouble, be arrested, and end up in jail one day."

After juvie, Joshua declared that Betty and I were no longer his family. His family were the thugs he hung out with. He didn't want anything to do with what we offered or what a better life offered. He saw career criminals as *his* people. They gave him self-worth.

◆ ◆ ◆

In May 1993, I met a woman named Sonya. She was a resident at a retirement facility for the infirm, one of my earliest HVAC clients.

She was an incredible woman with an insight into human nature and life. I adored her, and she adored me. "You're my favorite person on this whole planet, next to Snoopy," she told me frequently. "Yep, aside from Snoopy, you're my favorite person." She would get so excited whenever she saw me that she would slap me on my arms and chest like a little girl and tell me I was her barometer. "Look, look at those goosebumps on my arms—only you, only you. Damn you for making me feel this way. Nobody has this effect on me but you . . . You're my barometer because look at these goosebumps."

And she could look right through me. She saw through the façade of a poser directly to my pain, to the person I was. She knew my challenges without me having to confess them or share them with her. She could sense my voids and my needs, and so I always felt that I could be honest with her in ways that I couldn't with the other compartments in my life. Sonya resided in a space where, due to her intuition and my sense of openness with her, she saw it all. Or at least, most of it. She never lectured me. She just loved me. I felt safe, appreciated, and worthy with her in a way that I rarely, if ever, felt in other contexts with other people.

She also used to tell me, "I'm on a train, and sometimes people come on my train and get off at the next stop. Some stay on for more stops and some for less. But you, Mitchell, are going to be on my train until the last stop."

She was absolutely right. On May 31, 2009, acting as her guardian, I removed her from the elder facility and placed her in hospice care. A short while later, she died of cancer at age seventy-six.

At times, she'd tell me, "You're so sexy; you're so sexy; next lifetime, you're mine, bro!"

She didn't give a shit about what other people thought of her. She was herself and childlike in many ways, though she'd also lived through a lot of pain. She'd lost a son in a car crash while she was driving.

And she took a liking to Joshua. He took a liking to her, too. They'd met when Joshua was about eight, and Sonya was amazed at Joshua's maturity and intuitiveness. "He understands," she would say in terms of his knowing people and their feelings. "We can look in each other's eyes and have a conversation."

As a result, she doted on Joshua when he visited and treated him like a little man.

But despite this incredible person and her example, as well as that of Issa and many others, Joshua's life continued to fall apart. It was as if he was caught in a negative feedback loop that he couldn't escape. Just one bad choice after another, going deeper and deeper into violence, criminality, and drugs.

And then came Mother's Day 2006.

Joshua was the passenger of a car driven down Santa Monica Boulevard by his friend Butch. A police car passed them going the opposite direction but noticed either Joshua or Butch not wearing a seatbelt. The cops spun their car around and turned on the red and blues. Butch didn't make a run for it, but neither did he pull over immediately. He had a gun on him, and panicked by the cops, Butch tossed the gun out the window and then pulled over.

One of the cops walked back to retrieve the gun while the other told Butch and Joshua to get out of the car. With reasonable cause, the police officers called for backup and searched the car. Inside, the police found stolen wallets and—as the police later confirmed—clothes worn during the thefts. The police charged Butch and Joshua with five counts of armed robbery and assault with a weapon.

Butch and Joshua immediately started blaming each other for the crimes.

The court assigned a public defender to Joshua, and the prosecutor soon offered a plea deal: Admit to the crimes and each of them would get two strikes and a sentence of twelve years. Eighty-five percent of the sentence would be mandatory because a weapon was involved.

Joshua said he wouldn't admit to a crime he didn't commit.

I believed him. Did I believe that Joshua was guilty of poor judgment and stupidity? Absolutely. But a criminal? Not my son. Further, there was some evidence that Joshua wasn't involved. On at least one of the nights the robberies were committed, Betty confirmed that Joshua was at her house with a friend. Then, during the trial in June 2007, Joshua's attorney asked Joshua to stand so one of the victims could see him. "Do you recognize this person as the man who robbed you?" Joshua's attorney asked.

"I have never seen this man before," the victim said.

"Are you sure?" the lawyer asked.

"Yes. I'm sure."

The jury convicted Joshua for that robbery as an accomplice. The jury also convicted him for three of the other crimes.

Meanwhile, the evidence against Butch was overwhelming. Butch had stolen the gun from a neighbor. A security camera at a Denny's recorded Butch and his girlfriend paying for their meal with one of the victim's credit cards. All the physical evidence was in Butch's possession. There was not one piece of physical evidence or an eyewitness that could place Joshua at the scene of any of the crimes.

The judge took mercy on Joshua by sentencing him to the same deal originally offered by the prosecutor: twelve years, ten of those years mandatory without parole.

I was outraged that the system would railroad my son. I hired a new lawyer and appealed the case to California's Supreme Court. They rejected the appeal. I then appealed to the US Supreme Court. They denied the appeal. More than one hundred thousand dollars spent on legal fees, and game over.

Joshua was twenty years old. He would do the entire twelve years due to behavior issues in prison.

◆ ◆ ◆

When the police arrested Joshua, Issa was already dead, so when I told Sally, she'd just lost her husband and her brother. "Oh my gosh. Oh no. What happened? What did he do?"

What could I say but the truth? It was awful. Bad news after bad news that never gave Sally a break. At the same time, Yetty, Boris, and Toby were working her over for money. In a year, they'd abusively pressure her to sign the amendment to her will. That same year, 2007, beloved Ruska passed. Sally was the last of her family with the future of our wing of the family serving twelve years for armed robbery. This was one more sorrow on her list of complaints and emptiness that she expressed up to the day she died.

There is no doubt in my mind that Joshua was the inheritor of a legacy that began with the Holocaust. He was a third-generation survivor. I say this not to excuse my own behavior and responsibilities. What I am saying is that our family's inheritance of trauma did not end with me, as much as I promised myself it would. It took decades for me to finally find healthy coping tools so I could better navigate my life. No matter how well I kept all my vices/addictions compartment separate from the Joshua/fatherhood compartment, there was an effect, an impact, on Joshua. And so, the trauma I inherited sifted down to Joshua and became one piece of the total negative impacts of his life.

Given my own state of acting out and poor life navigating, I did all that was possible for me to do for my son. And even as Joshua entered prison, I was compartmentalizing, still fully engaged with each compartment. Lee and chaos: full on. Career: full on. Looking after Sally: full on.

Parent: full on. Sadly, and tragically, this last compartment was the one where the other participant wanted nothing to do with me and the values that I tried to inculcate in him. He wanted nothing to do with what Betty and her family offered, either.

◆ ◆ ◆

During his incarceration, there were moments when Joshua gave us hope.

Sonya would write to Joshua, and Joshua would respond. And despite Joshua's very hard exterior, it felt like Sonya could touch the insightful and intuitive child that still existed within him. I hoped the love of this special woman, someone with a unique understanding of life, would help Joshua open up with me. I wanted him to talk to me, tell me from his perspective whatever I did wrong. I wanted to hear it. I wanted him to give me the chance to apologize and resolve our issues. I wanted him to be open and honest, to scream at me, but he never did. He knew that I wanted these things, so perhaps he withheld them as a way to be in control and cause me pain.

Sonya once said, "The child remains with us, no matter what age." I took this to mean that we carry within us the same aspirations and hopes and desire for peace and stability into adulthood. And therefore, we also carry the same disappointments, fears, and instabilities into adulthood if they instill themselves into our childhood. I'm sure she wrote this to Joshua as both a plea to him and a plea for him to accept me as I was, not as he wished me to be.

Sonya was the only person who knew Joshua and me to our core. Her love for us was deep because she saw our better angels lurking within. That line—*the child remains with us*—is one of the greatest gifts ever given to me.

Another moment of hope came when, due to the overpopulation crisis in California's prisons, Joshua volunteered in 2011 for the state to relocate him to a private prison in Mississippi. The entire population at this prison were California inmate transplants. I was proud of him for making this choice. He would move far away from so many of the people he knew, not just his family but also the friends and fellow inmates who were such a bad influence. He also knew the conditions in this prison would be an improvement to the shithole conditions in California.

The first time Betty and I visited him, we were pleasantly surprised by how the guards treated us. They seemed genuinely happy to see us at every visit we made, telling us how important visitors were to the inmates and how visits reduced the tension in the entire facility. Still, they were guards, and this was prison.

Two years later, in 2013, the system transferred Joshua to another private facility in Oklahoma. At this prison, he decided to excommunicate himself from the gang system inside the prison. This was a huge and risky decision that was a positive step for any inmate. Once an inmate makes this statement, the prison must transfer that inmate to a special ward for the remainder of their incarceration to protect them.

However, Joshua still enjoyed torturing Betty and me. His biggest point of leverage was getting tattoos. They were illegal to get in prison, but it was a meaningless prohibition. Joshua loved taunting us with the tattoos he had—all violence- and gang-related—and the ones he planned to get.

And he was still a hard person. He was required to serve ten and a half years in prison and could have been released after that time. But due to his number of write-ups—similar to prison demerits for breaking rules—and outright violent behavior, the state judicial system required that he serve all twelve of his years. For three quarters of his incarceration, his anger and attitude did not change. The only sign of change was when he wanted out of the prison gang world in Oklahoma.

◆ ◆ ◆

As he neared release, Joshua began to share his mixed emotions about joining the outside world. He told us that he had doubts about being ready. After about six months of that, he started to feel more at ease with getting out. We would talk about all the things he could do with his life afterward.

And then, the release date went from something that felt distant to an impending reality. The prison system transferred him back to a prison in California nearer to Betty and me. His release date was January 31, 2019. The September before that, Betty and I visited Joshua. As we sat with him, he showed us his latest tattoos, which he knew we would find disturbing. The tattoos were not more than a month old, with one showing a man with a gun in front of his face and his mouth covered with a handkerchief, like a robber. The other was a cynical, joker-looking face with a gun barrel. I also noticed that tattooed on three of Joshua's fingers were the numbers 2-1-1, police code for armed robbery.

"What is this?" I asked. "Some sort of badge of honor for everyone to see?"

His eyes flared. "No, of course not."

"Doesn't this just glorify violence, a gang lifestyle?"

He placed one hand down hard on the table. Not hard enough to be loud, but hard enough to show his anger. He rejected what I said, then he admitted that he and Butch did rob those five people at gunpoint.

"Yeah, I wasn't innocent," he said.

I looked at him, as sadness and frustration welled up in my eyes. "Was the gun loaded?"

"Yes."

We sat in silence for a minute, maybe two.

"I think it's time for us to go," I said.

"Yeah, I think it is," Joshua agreed.

We stood. Betty hugged Joshua hard, with abundant love, sadness, and despair.

I struggled with what to tell him as I hugged him. With my mouth close to his ear, I said, "Son, I'm not judging you. Do you hear me? I'm not judging you."

Except for the radio, Betty and I were silent the entire four-hour ride home, both of us on the verge of tears. Both of us in despair for our son. I was also ashamed and disgusted that my son could be so cruel and heartless toward another human being.

This was the state of my feelings when the prison system released Joshua on January 30, 2019.

◆ ◆ ◆

After his release, Joshua entered a halfway house where he enrolled in a culinary school. Prior to his arrest, Joshua had shown an interest in culinary school, even attending one for a short while. With prison behind him, he made it to the top of his culinary class. He also seemed motivated and hopeful about his prospects—the most committed to finding a better life than I'd ever seen him.

This lasted about four months. In a random drug test in May 2019, he tested positive for drugs. This broke his parole, and the halfway house sent him to Riverside County Jail. At his court hearing, the judge gave him a choice: serve a three-year sentence or enroll in a Salvation Army rehabilitation center in Orange County for one year.

He chose the latter, which was a strict program that a high percentage of enrollees found too difficult to finish and were sent back to jail.

I visited Joshua after his first month at the Salvation Army rehabilitation facility, expecting to see an angry person who'd given up on himself. Instead, I hadn't seen him so playful and filled with energy in a very long time. We were able to go out to eat and see a movie. *This is the old Josh*, I thought.

Before I left him at the rehab center, he asked for a package of hygiene products, the best I could get. I knew he would use these to barter for cigarettes, which I hated. I waited a month, then sent the package with the strongest letter of love and encouragement I could write. *I believe in you, that you are truly good, and I love you, very much* was the sentiment at the heart of what I wrote.

◆ ◆ ◆

Nine months after Joshua's release, I was sitting in a restaurant bar drinking a martini. The bar was upscale, so my drink came with a fancy olive stuffed with bleu cheese.

One of the miracles of getting free of Lee was that I'd never become dependent or addicted to alcohol. I depended on alcohol when I was in Lee's physical presence, but not after we'd split for the last time New Year's Eve 2011. I spent some time sober, but as I learned more about myself, my triggers, how to be a happier person, I came to realize that alcohol had no great pull on me. I could drink one drink, or less, and walk away.

"Are you going to eat that olive?" I turned to see a woman with an alluring voice and confident demeanor nodding toward the olive I'd set on a napkin next to my drink, a fancy toothpick skewering it.

"My name's Marie," she said. Obviously, I'd gone dumb for a moment. "That olive, are you going to eat it?"

She wore an elegant black dress and just a touch of makeup. What stood out most was the casual ease with which she made such a forward request of a stranger.

I said, "Yes."

Despite six years of freedom from Lee and a lot of therapy with Ann and self-help to help me do the hard work of healing, the past seven years had not built my self-esteem with women. There were flings that ended quickly, sometimes painfully. Somehow, I always came to these prospective relationships thinking, *Why me?*

Why would any woman want me unless I paid her or she wanted to engage in a toxic, mutually self-destructive relationship with me? I took it for granted that I was unworthy and undeserving of love.

"Oh," Marie said. "A lot of people often just leave them. They're really good."

I cringed as I realized Marie actually wanted to talk to me more than she wanted the olive. The old me would have accepted that I'd blown an opportunity that presented itself in such a random and delightful manner; I would have accepted it as part of the game and moved on. I'd spent most of my life developing strategies to keep from exposing my flaws, weaknesses, and fears. With Ann's help, I was learning to step through my flaws. As she had said often, "To deal with any of your issues, Mitchell, involves a crucial first step. You must confront them. Hiding from them only makes them bigger. They fester and breed. They become monsters under your bed."

"You can have the olive, actually," I told Marie.

Marie smiled. "Thank you."

We began to chat. I ordered another round, one for her and one for me . . . and I gave her my fancy olive. She said, "Thank you, Mitchell."

I was surprised when a few minutes later Marie's friend said she had to go, and Marie decided to stay. I was also surprised that she agreed to give me her number. But I was stunned when she agreed to have dinner with me the next Friday.

During the hour or so that we spent sharing a drink, I searched her eyes and face for any indication of the person behind them, and I believed Marie to be lighthearted and candid. There was nothing threatening or belittling about her. She was striking and wholesome in a way that caught my fullest attention.

It was the beginning of a conversation that has lasted to this writing.

◆ ◆ ◆

November went quickly, as did December. Marie and I went from dating on weekends to spending more time together during the week, and she became the new person in my life. Though I managed to push through my fears, I told Marie I was not good at being in a relationship and warned her that I would manage to fuck up ours somehow, someway, and I did.

Marie and I had our first fight. It was inevitable because I'm me, and Marie is a strong and confident person. Plus, relationships do this.

She became upset as we quarreled and left. I thought she had left as in gone, over. But really, she just wanted to cool down.

We had planned a trip together for my birthday, so the next morning I canceled the trip and sent her a text to let her know.

Her reply: *Very hurtful, Mitchell!*

Huh? What? Wait a minute. Until that moment, I didn't think she took me seriously, but here she was, hurt by my actions. The text was endearing and raw because before I received it, I believed she couldn't possibly care about a guy like me. I didn't think I could hurt her. Instead of being nasty, she expressed her feelings and let me know how I made her feel.

We're supposed to have feelings here?

Of course, yes.

Without her three words—*Very hurtful, Mitchell!*—I don't believe we'd still be together. I would have just let her walk away because I would have believed that's what I deserved. It was the nature of the game.

Instead, I learned one of the most incredible lessons of my life:

Creating chaos is not how to love someone or how someone should love you back.

Marie is so absolutely disarming and wonderful at making me feel comfortable in my own skin. The only other person who could do that had been Issa. Marie is not the new Issa, however; she is something new entirely.

◆ ◆ ◆

New Year's Eve approached—always a loaded night—and Marie and I made plans for our first trip together. We decided on San Francisco. It was absolutely lovely.

The next morning, around nine, we sat in our rental car talking about how to spend the couple of hours before our flight back to Los Angeles. My phone rang. It was Betty.

"The police are here, Mitchell." Tears choked her words. "Joshua's dead."

Staff—or maybe it was a resident—at the Salvation Army rehabilitation center last saw Joshua on the afternoon of December 31, 2019, leaving the center's grounds with a backpack. He was running away, an automatic parole violation that would trigger the marshals' response and send him back to prison. In the early hours of the next morning, two men exited a car and dumped Joshua's body in front of the emergency room of a hospital in Riverside. An ER doctor pronounced Joshua dead. The doctor then determined it was due to a drug overdose.

I was in shock. "Okay," I said to Betty, not sure what else to say.

Marie could hear the conversation. She leaned toward me to comfort me and began to cry. She'd not yet met Joshua.

"I'll be home later today," I told Betty.

When we hung up, I called Betty's neighbor to sit with her and make sure she was physically all right. She'd had an issue with her heart a few years before that required a pacemaker. I was worried this shock could cause her to have a cardiac issue.

After that, I held Marie—or probably more likely, she held me—but I didn't cry. I was in shock but also calm. I'd always known that this outcome was as likely as any other, but that never meant I lost hope, especially since Joshua seemed to have found the will to transform his life.

I started calling people to let them know Joshua had died. I wanted to avoid their calls of sympathy and just get it over with.

Marie and I made it back to Los Angeles. I never saw Joshua's body; the coroner had taken it away. It took me a few weeks to summon the courage to go to Joshua's grave.

I loved my son. I loved him even after he pointed a loaded gun at another person's head to rob them. But I did not like him. I did not like that he'd become cruel and desensitized to causing such suffering and fear. The way his life turned out was a huge disappointment to me. I take some responsibility for that, and I regret that I couldn't be a better parent to myself much less Joshua. I never abused him, and I did what I could to give him the best possible life. But I deeply regret some of the decisions I made.

As I now reflect back in time, not long after my son was born, one of my sisters-in-law gave me a page that she had torn out of a magazine. She did not say much other than, "I read this and thought of you, being a new father and all." The first time I read the poem, it touched me deeply, as it has every time since.

One Small Child

What shall you give to one small child?
A glamorous game, a tinseled toy,
A puzzle pack, a life-like doll,
A picture book, a real live pet . . .

No, there's plenty of time for such things yet.
Give them a day for their very own . . .
Just one small child and their dad alone.
A walk in the woods, a romp in the park,
A fishing trip from dawn to dark,
Give the gift that only you can—
The companionship of their Old Man.
Games are outgrown, and toys decay—
But they'll never forget if you—
"Give them a day"

—author unknown

I had the page converted into a poster and hung it in every home I lived in for the next thirty years. It was one of the most cherished objects that I owned, and I had hoped to pass it along to Joshua when he became a father of his own.

I should have kept Joshua and Lee separate and focused on Joshua. I believe Joshua always felt like he was competing with Lee for my affection and attention.

I was twenty-six when Betty and I married. I was immature, naive, and acting out in incredibly unhealthy ways. I was too young and too damaged. I am responsible for my decisions. Like Joshua, I could have chosen a less destructive path, healthier coping tools so that I could better navigate life, but I didn't.

That I *had* to choose healthier coping skills to better navigate my life is something I am still remorseful over. Not everyone is born with that responsibility.

Not everyone while riding a tricycle at age four hears a strange woman call out, "Little boy, I know your name."

◆ ◆ ◆

Meeting Marie was a significant catalyst for my desire to change.

One of my problems—thank you, Ann, for helping identify it—is that I have a lot of emotion, but I don't show it or do a good job of explaining how I feel. After Joshua's death, I should have cried. I should have cried for days, weeks even, but there was nothing, not one tear.

I stopped seeing Ann in 2013 for a range of reasons, all of them good and reasonable, though I'd check in with her from time to time, mostly through email. So, when I couldn't cry and felt so numb, I sought out a local therapist.

I sat in her office and told her my story, from the ground up. I ended with Joshua's body in front of the emergency room.

"I haven't cried," I said. "I feel numb. Why?"

She thought for a moment. Then, "You lost your son years ago, when he was seventeen."

"Yes. Aha. That's true. Great. Thanks. I don't need to come back. I have the answer, and it makes sense."

But life's never that simple. She gave me an answer. Maybe it's *the* correct answer. No matter, I felt better even as the pain and disappointment lingered on.

◆ ◆ ◆

Today, I love myself more than I ever have.

When I told Ann that Marie and I were engaged and how happy I was, she called back to say that in her forty-year career as a therapist, I was her most successful client. "Given all you've been through, I'm near tears," she said.

To this day, I want to do better. I want to know when I make mistakes with Marie.

And I look at my son and the path he went down that led to his death. The fact is that his demise should have been my demise. This is why, when I tell my story, I often start or end it with "I should be dead or at least a derelict or in prison, or all of the above." However, I pulled through everything, and I live a good life now. At age sixty-four, I have achieved—with the help of Marie's ability to understand and support me—my lifetime goal of becoming the man I always wanted to be but did not know how.

The truth is, I am a son without parents, a father without a son. There is no one to carry on my family's name, to be my heir, to provide a grandchild, to prove that the cycle of trauma has ended. But what is truly unbearable is that I'd dreamed of the day when Joshua would come to me and say, "Dad, I'm so sorry for all I've put you and Mom through. Now that I'm a father too, I get it. Please forgive me."

Of course I would . . . if he'd only lived long enough to give me the chance.

Joshua and me—given that I was still wearing my HVAC uniform,
I must have just gotten home.

My sister visiting me in my new apartment during my divorce from Betty—
Malka's look of rapture being with her brother is priceless.

Sonya at Joshua's
bar mitzvah

My father around his
late sixties—the look
of a broken man

Malka and me—this photo was taken less than a year before her untimely death. During the photo shoot, she was hesitant to put her hand on my shoulder when the photographer instructed her to do so.

She was apprehensive due to me being a man and her being ultra-orthodox. She began talking to herself out loud while she was standing by my side saying, "Well, I think it's permitted since he is my brother."

Le' chaim

EPILOGUE

MY LIFE, TO SAY THE LEAST, has been one of tumult, but after four decades, I've finally managed to firmly place myself on the right track of happiness and some form of peace within myself. Simply put, I am comfortable in my own skin.

Given everything that I have endured, it amazes me that I did not end up becoming an angry, violent person. Instead, I was able to overcome all my addictions and vices—whether substances or toxic relationships—and find a new life with a wonderful and caring woman. Marie has shown me how to be vulnerable and how to truly love for the first time in my life.

This memoir was originally meant to help my son find his way in life as a young man. It was my hope that he would have learned from his old man that no one is perfect, including and especially his dad. It's my greatest pain that he did not live to heal and read these words as a stable and loving adult. But that does not mean one should ever stop trying to find a better way to be comfortable in one's own skin.

My hope is that my story will inspire others to not give up when their lives feel hopeless, and they feel there is nothing to live for. I have a saying that I live by and share with others every chance I get: No matter how overwhelming your problems seem, be grateful for them—the stranger next to you may have it a whole lot worse, and they would be more than willing to trade places with you in a heartbeat.

We also never know where healing, love, and a desire to be better will lead us. For the past twelve years, I have been involved with a nonprofit Christian ministry that serves and distributes clothing and accessories to the homeless of Orange County. For the past seven years, I have been the director of this Christian ministry. It really amuses me that, with my Jewish background, I am running a Christian ministry. I am so proud of the diversity of it all. It has been a dream come true for me to be in a position where I am able to lead so many fellow volunteers in helping the direst in our society without judgment or prejudice.

And so, in my current life, Marie loves me. She's a college-educated, independent, strong, smarter than smart, beautiful, rational woman who loves me and wants to be my wife. The lead pastor of the Christian ministry recently said, "Mitchell, you're my hero."

When writing a story such as this, it's impossible to include every person who has made a difference in my life. In particular, I want to thank the Mizrachi family for their love, generosity, and kindness. When I was a scared child who had recently run away from his abusive mother, the Mizrachis accepted and welcomed me as one of their own. Then, throughout my life—especially when living in or visiting Israel—they always welcomed me with love. They were and remain an incredible example of what family is and should be all about.

I love you all for being in a special place in my heart.

Thank you.

ABOUT THE AUTHOR

 **MITCHELL RAFF** is a second-generation Holocaust survivor who grew up in Los Angeles. As a child, he was kidnapped and taken to Israel where he lived for a year and a half before the private investigator hired by his family located him. This led to a lifelong connection with the Jewish homeland, and as a young man, he returned to Israel to serve in the Israeli Defense Force. A former business owner, Mitchell now resides in Southern California and is the owner and director of an outreach charity, Clothing the Homeless. *Little Boy, I Know Your Name: A Second-Generation Memoir from Inherited Holocaust Trauma* is his first book, and it is an intensely personal examination of how he survived being the child of survivors.